D1348914

A TALE OF THREE CITIES

By the same Author

THE BUSINESS OF MUSIC

A
TALE OF
THREE CITIES

ERNST ROTH

CASSELL · LONDON

CASSELL & COMPANY LTD
35 Red Lion Square, London WC1
Melbourne, Sydney, Toronto
Johannesburg, Auckland

© Ernst Roth 1971
All rights reserved. No part of this publication
may be reproduced, stored in a retrieval system,
or transmitted, in any form or by any means,
electronic, mechanical, photocopying, recording
or otherwise, without the prior permission of
Cassell and Company Ltd.

First published 1971

I.S.B.N. 0 304 93701 0

Printed in Great Britain by
The Camelot Press Ltd., London and Southampton

F.1170

Contents

MAPS

Introduction

I must ask the reader's indulgence for the 'capsulated' history and geography in the following pages. But meeting many otherwise well-informed people in the West—and the West, in this context, stretches from the Rhine to the Pacific coast of America —I have been amazed how little is known of the past and of the peoples who once formed the Austro-Hungarian Empire.

At a university panel game in London not long ago, eight undergraduates from Oxford and Cambridge were asked: 'Where is the Iron Gate?', and only one hazarded an answer: in Spain. Alas, I thought, from what forlorn corner of the earth have I come? These learned young men knew all about the Nicobars, Kinshasa and Kampala, but had never heard of the Iron Gate!

I would not be so bold as to suggest that the Iron Gate or any other place in former Austro-Hungary is an indispensable part of general knowledge; but in writing of that vanished world in which I grew up, I felt that the tale would be incomplete and often incomprehensible without the background, however sketchily presented, to the past.

I would refer the reader to the two maps on pages x and xi. Together, they represent incomparable examples of the political and ethnic absurdities of which the human race is capable. Yet who is to say that the Habsburg Empire bore within it greater seeds of destruction than those which were sown by the political cartographers of Versailles and Trianon? At least it lasted for 650 years which, by imperial standards, is unique.

I hope, therefore, that the reader will bear with me and that my historical digressions will help to bring to life the peoples of that strange empire who are the main theme of this book.

Notes on the Maps

The two maps on the following pages show the same area of Europe on the outbreak of the First World War and the year after the 'Collapse' in 1918. Though they are separated in time by only five years, they illustrate the shifting sands of several centuries.

Map A shows the Austro-Hungarian Empire as it was in 1914, outlined in red. I have indicated Hungary as 'a kingdom within an empire'—as indeed it was. Place names are those in common usage under the Empire.

Map B shows the Successor States which came into existence after the 'Collapse' and the post-War political settlement. I have superimposed upon this map, in red outline, the pre-War frontiers of the old Empire so that the reader may recognize at a glance the extensive—and often absurd—adjustments made by the post-War politicians. Place names in *Map B* are given in both their new and old style and so far as possible I have included identical detail in both maps.

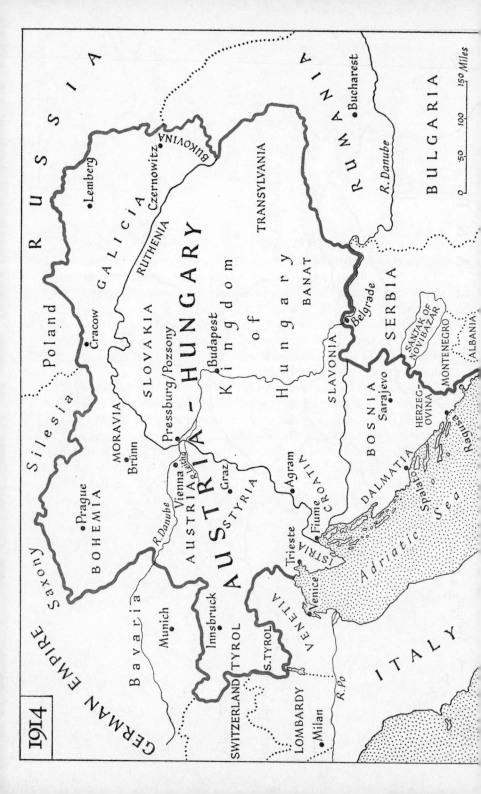

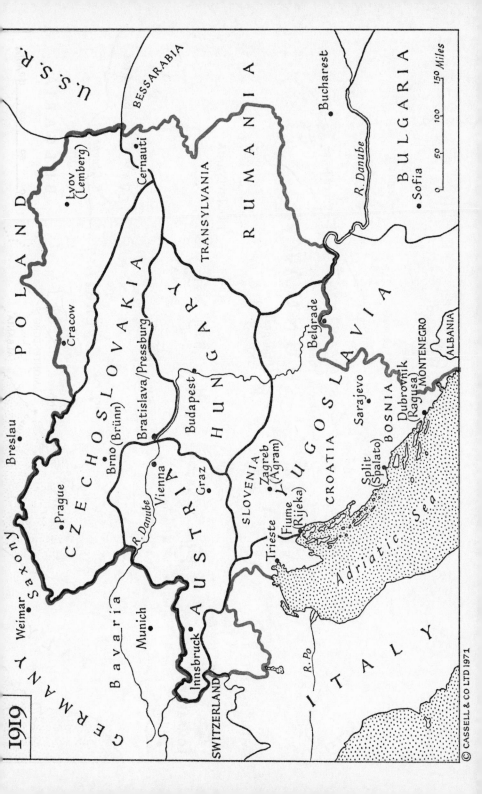

1919

GERMANY

Weimar

Saxony

Breslau

POLAND

U.S.S.R.

Cracow

Lyov (Lemberg)

Prague

CZECHOSLOVAKIA

Cernauti

BESSARABIA

Brno (Brünn)

Bratislava/Pressburg

Bavaria

R. Danube

Vienna

Munich

AUSTRIA

Graz

Budapest

HUNGARY

TRANSYLVANIA

RUMANIA

Bucharest

BULGARIA

Sofia

R. Danube

Innsbruck

SWITZERLAND

SLOVENIA

Zagreb (Agram)

Fiume (Rijeka)

Trieste

R. Po

ITALY

YUGOSLAVIA

Belgrade

CROATIA

Sarajevo

BOSNIA

Split (Spalato)

Dubrovnik (Ragusa)

MONTENEGRO

ALBANIA

Adriatic Sea

0   50   100   150 Miles

© CASSELL & CO LTD 1971

Once upon a time . . .

It sounds almost like a fairy-tale. Once upon a time, when I was young, there was a great empire in the very heart of Europe, a collection of a dozen colourful nations, some of them almost unknown to the world at large, all of them united and divided, happy and dissatisfied, presided over by an imperial court of imperial splendour. And one day it was all swept away leaving nothing but a sentimental and sometimes absurd tale to be told by the nostalgic old to the unbelieving young: the tale of the Danube, the Habsburg, the Double Monarchy.

Has this land of make-believe really disappeared without a trace like Atlantis submerged in the ocean of history?

Not long ago a curious traveller, who himself knew the fairy-land from books and hearsay only, set out on a journey through all the former provinces of the Monarchy in search of any remnants of the past. It was no easy journey. Our traveller needed a passport and many visas, he had to cross many frontiers and change his money many times where—once upon a time—no passports, visas, frontiers and currencies were thought of. But now Austrian and Czechoslovak, Polish and Russian, Hungarian and Rumanian, Yugoslav and Italian frontier police checked his papers and customs officers rummaged in his luggage.

However, he considered himself amply rewarded. More than fifty years after what was everywhere simply called the 'Collapse', there were still traces of the olden days. Somewhere in a Galician, now Polish, town they had forgotten to obliterate the name of a grammar school and one could still read the name 'k. k. Franz Josephs-Gymnasium'. In the former capital of the former dukedom of Bukovina, 'the Beech Tree Country', once Austrian Czernowitz, then Rumanian Cernauti, now Russian

I

Tchernowtzy, an old lady still kept the white dress uniform of her grandfather who had been a general in the Austrian army. In Budapest everybody spoke of 'Elizabeth Bridge', named after the Empress Elizabeth. In the south-east where the Danube once separated Austrians and Turks, the old fortresses still stood with their bastions and embrasures pointing south—in the wrong direction, for now the country all round is Yugoslavia. And in Prague an old man told the inquisitive traveller: 'I always dreamed of joining the navy—but where is the sea now?'

Unfortunately all these are trivialities. Those who spoke of the old Austria, sometimes with a tear in their eye, spoke like children who have lost a toy. Nobody could really tell of any positive achievement of Austrian rule. Nobody seemed proud of having been Austrian, but rather ashamed and secretly or overtly sorry for no apparent reason.

This is very strange. Austrian rule was no doubt an eminently civilizing force among peoples on the fringe of Europe. It lasted altogether nearly 650 years, longer than any other rule in the Western world. At one time, when the Turks came, the fate of Christianity depended on the Habsburg Empire. Should it not have earned some modest measure of gratitude and respect?

One cannot help thinking of the ancient Romans who conquered and ruled the barbarians for barely 400 years. They could be very harsh; their enemies, Queen Boadicea, Vercingetorix, Hermann the Cheruscan, are remembered as freedom fighters. But from the Atlantic to the Black Sea the descendants of all those who once held Roman citizenship are proud of their 'Latinity'. The French, because of it, feel superior to the Germans; and the Germans West of the Rhine feel superior to those East of the river. And, after all, the Roman Empire collapsed no less ignominiously than the Austrian. But Roman virtues outshone and outlasted their many vices and no curious traveller needs to search for Roman relics among the rubbish in an attic. They are reverently exhibited in museums, and every town and village treasures the piece of Roman masonry that may have been unearthed within its precincts. In contrast, and with the exception of present-day Austria itself, Austrian relics and reminders have been destroyed, defaced or hidden like old sins.

This, surely, is a mark of total failure. No Frenchman blushes when remembering Henry IV, Louis XIV or Napoleon whose monuments and memories have survived the Terror and the Commune. But none of the twenty-two Habsburg kings and emperors has endeared himself to all or even to most of his many peoples. There was no really bad man or woman among them. The historian Jacob Burckhardt, as a Swiss traditionally out of sympathy with the Habsburgs, wrote this about them: 'Their physique was not ideal, they had little ingenuity, but they had good intentions, they were serious and thoughtful, persevering and steadfast in adversity, neither dissolutes nor villains.' The nicknames given to them by their contemporaries are significant: 'The Wise', 'The Lame', 'The Founder', 'The Handsome', 'The Jolly', 'The Last Knight', 'The Benevolent'. One was even sympathetically called 'Freddie with the empty pocket'. But there was no 'Cruel' or 'Bloody' or 'Conqueror' among them nor any 'Great'; which ought to be particularly gratifying for the 'Great' are the most suspect characters in history. However, with all their good qualities they would have made exemplary citizens, shopkeepers, farmers, but not good dukes or emperors or kings.

Anti-Habsburg historians—and most historians seem to be anti-Habsburg—would say that, out of greed, the Habsburgs collected a harlequin set of countries and nations by schemes and tricks and with complete disregard of historic values; and that, therefore, the 'Collapse' and their banishment were their just reward.

But was this harlequin set of nations really so artificial as modern opinion suggests? In the region called the Danube Basin, populated by an odd assortment of small nations who did not seem to have anything in common, there was an almost mysterious gravitational force which tended to draw them together. The Habsburgs were neither the only nor the first to have felt the pull of that force. In the thirteenth century a Bohemian, in the fifteenth a Hungarian king, created an empire reaching from the Saxon border in the North to the Adriatic in the South, so anticipating the Austro-Hungarian Monarchy. But only the Habsburgs eventually succeeded, for they had an inestimable advantage over their competitors: the centre of gravity could be neither Prague nor Budapest but only the place where the roads from North to South, from East to West crossed: Vienna. And Vienna was firmly in Habsburg hands. Moreover, historic values are a fairly recent discovery. In the formative days of the Habsburg Empire they did not count for much. Countries were bought and sold and inherited like real estate, stocks and shares today.

The Habsburgs were no pioneers by inclination. They had their eyes fixed on the more inviting and more manageable West. But once their Western plans miscarried they accepted the historic task of 'Europeanizing' Europe's South-East and they fulfilled it with little violence in spite of their reputation of having been oppressors. They were indeed proud of the 'inborn clemency of the arch-house' as one of them expressed it. As a result, they failed to create an Austrian nation. The merciless de- and re-nationalization practised in Prussia or Russia or even in Hungary never took place in Austria proper. The Habsburgs were certainly Germans or, more accurately, Swiss Germans. For five hundred years on and off they were kings and emperors of Germany. But German, like any other nationalism, was alien to them. If, in the eighteenth century, German was made the state language, replacing Latin, it was due to the growing complexity of administration which could not be carried on in eleven different languages. But there was no attempt at forcible Germanization.

However, there was not only the 'clementia Austriaca' but also the 'pietas Austriaca', the unswerving adherence of the arch-house to the Catholic faith. It was this 'pietas' which has tended to stain their memory. The Roman Catholic faith was Habsburg's most sensitive spot, sensitive to the point of intolerance. For the greater glory of God they could even become violent and cruel and it made no difference to them whether Protestants were German, Czech or Hungarian. At the point of 'pietas' their 'clementia' almost vanished. And those who suffered never forgave them.

The Habsburg 'pietas' had yet another equally unpopular side. To their last day, certainly to the last day of Emperor Franz Joseph who died on November 21, 1916, the Habsburgs firmly believed in their divine mission to rule. To rule was not only their privilege; it was, first and foremost, a duty thrust upon them by providence. This was certainly a respectable attitude and they took it literally and seriously. But it was incapable of 'modernization', incapable of adapting itself to change. When, after the Napoleonic wars, the ideas both of nationalism and of democracy began to develop, the Habsburgs found themselves more and more out of tune with the times. How could a divine mission be shared with anyone? How could a divine task be delegated? The Habsburgs had to fight revolution, execute revolutionaries. A constitution had to be wrested from them, but they stubbornly retained the ill-famed Clause 14 which left it to the discretion of the emperor to declare a state of emergency, adjourn parliament *sine die* and rule without it. To them this was as logical as it was fatal. When the great crisis came in 1914 there was no parliament, no consultation. The emperor alone signed the declaration of war, the death warrant of his empire and of his dynasty. 'Tyranny tempered by negligence' a Viennese member of parliament called the Habsburgs' dilemma.

The gravitational force in the Danube Basin was still at work in the nineteenth century. The Croat general who with 20,000 Croats quelled the rising in Vienna in 1848 justified his intervention by asserting that the Monarchy was a necessity for all its members and for Europe. And when, in 1866, he could have destroyed it with a stroke of his pen, Bismarck proclaimed that the multi-national and multi-racial Monarchy would have to be invented if it did not exist already. But a new era had dawned, an era of industrialization and technology. In that part of the world it was slow in coming but it cast a warning shadow ahead of it. Its innermost meaning was to invalidate natural conditions, to make the moon or the bottom of the sea habitable for man. And this mere premonition already loosened the grip of the old gravitational force. Hidden in all the squabbles of the last decades of the Monarchy was the feeling that the old interdependence of its eleven nations was no longer a necessity and that these nations—and Europe—could well do without the Austro-Hungarian Empire.

When eventually the moment of truth arrived, the unimaginable happened: the Monarchy 'collapsed'. It was no dramatic coup. The old house just fell apart. Nobody seriously tried to save it. There was no fighting in the streets, there were no farewell parties. The Habsburgs were not overthrown; they were dismissed like redundant servants. Though they had never done enough to be generally hated, they had not done enough to be generally loved. A German diplomat at the time noted in his diary: 'The Habsburgs ended like gentlemen, the Hohenzollern like coachmen.' Indeed, the Habsburgs were politely complimented to the door and the British paid the last emperor's fare to Madeira.

At long last there was the opportunity for new happiness in the Danube Basin. The nations were free, their supposed oppressors had gone. But, alas, the new happiness did not spread as rapidly and as readily as had been expected. Confusion and disorder were complete. Innumerable threads were broken and hundreds of thousands found themselves 'abroad' where, the day before, they had been at home. Austria proper and Vienna in particular were left bewildered, destitute, disorganized. The Hungarians who had for so long and so vehemently clamoured for independence lost almost two-thirds of their country and complained in vain that their former 'guests', the Slovaks, Rumanians, Croats and Slovenes, had made themselves masters. Croats and Slovenes, now united with the Serbs in the new kingdom SHS,* found Serbian rule no more to their taste than the Habsburg crown, and a Croat shot a Serbian king. The Poles in Galicia and Lodomeria had no choice but to embrace their brethren from former Western Prussia and from the former Russian 'Gouvernement Warsaw' and remembered sadly the happy days of the 'Polish Club' in Vienna. The Italians disbanded the 'Irredenta', the organization for the liberation of Italian territory, and celebrated their reunion with their kith and kin; but the resorts in Southern Tyrol, or 'Alto Adige' as they called the new province, the promenades of Abbazia and Laurana, the beaches of Grado were deserted and the quais and warehouses of Trieste stood empty for lack of a hinterland, while Yugoslav frontier guards looked down on the sun-soaked bay. Only the Czechs were unquestionably satisfied. They inherited most of the old empire's industry whose headquarters had to move from Vienna to Prague which grew and became a capital city once more. There alone was the prosperity which had so confidently been expected by all the successor states.

* Srpsko – Horvatsko – Slovensko = Yugoslavia

6

However, history itself was to write a melancholy postscript to the fairy-tale of the old Monarchy. After centuries of common troubles and common peace, the peoples of the old Monarchy were to have barely twenty years of the freedom they had longed for. When the new storm broke, all the little states and nations of the Danube Basin were involved and engulfed, trodden underfoot without protection, choice or hope. The discarded gravitational force took a terrible revenge. And the new catastrophe has about it the bleak trappings of finality.

VIENNA AND THE AUSTRIANS

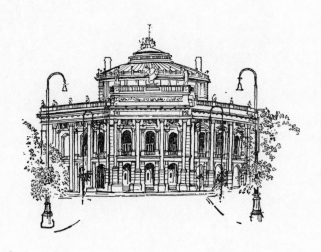

I

The Danube, Habsburg or Double Monarchy

The official description of the Austrian Empire at the beginning of this century was 'The Imperial and Royal Austro-Hungarian Monarchy'. That was good and pompous enough for official documents but not suitable for daily use. People in all the 'crown lands' preferred to speak of the Danube, Habsburg or Double Monarchy.

'Danube Monarchy' was fairly obvious, although not quite accurate. The Danube certainly was the most conspicuous feature and, as it were, the spine of the Monarchy. But there were large provinces far away from the Danube which, hydrographically, belonged to other river systems. This affected not only their geography, but also their outlook and their sympathies. Nor was the Austro-Hungarian the only Danube monarchy. There were five others between the Black Forest where the Danube has its source and the Black Sea where it empties its waters. However, the Austro-Hungarian was the largest of them all and if one thought of the Danube one thought instinctively of Austria and Hungary, of Vienna and Budapest.

The Danube is a mighty stream. If one withholds European status from the Volga, it is the largest in Europe. In its course of over two thousand miles it crosses or skirts ten different countries, listens to six different languages—not counting mere dialects—has six different though not dissimilar names. This disqualifies it as a 'national' river. None of the many nations which live on its banks can claim it as 'their' river. But it suffers from an even more serious setback. The Rhine, its most obvious rival, flows North and West into the open sea, into the wide world which kindles the spirit of adventure and makes people aggressive and haughty. But the Danube stubbornly flows East, in the 'wrong' direction, to the other side of Europe, to the land-locked Black Sea and to the shores of old Tauris of which already the ancient Greeks thought uneasily, a place of exile for Roman poets in which to write their tearful lamentations. On the Piazza Navona in Rome you can see the Danube in the exotic company of the Nile, Ganges and La Plata. But it is the odd one out. The other three come *from* the unknown, the Danube flows *towards* the unknown. In 1651, when the 'Four River Fountain' was erected, it was lost in the Ottoman Empire. And today, no less than two thousand years ago, one follows its course with apprehension rather than expectation.

However, the Danube starts merrily and hopefully in Württemberg amidst the green hills of the Black Forest, amply nourished by the waters of the Alps which, one by one, accelerate its current and widen its bed and give it strength to cut its way through the hills when, opposite the old bishopric of Passau, it enters Austria. There all is rural idyll and romance, green hills on both banks with vineyards on the slopes, splendid baroque abbeys or picturesque ruins of mediaeval castles on the summits and old towns and villages huddled together on the narrow shelves between hill and river. Experienced travellers would say that the stretch of the Danube between Linz, the capital of Upper Austria, and Vienna is more beautiful than the Rhine between Mainz and Bonn. It speaks for the friendlier disposition of the Danube people that their fancy populates their river with thoroughly likeable nymphs with an innocent predilection for waltzes, instead of the golden-haired, vengeful Lorelei who lures credulous fishermen to her rock and to their doom in the Rhine. Indeed, the Rhine always incited raucous drinking or provocative war songs while the Danube songs were sweet, nostalgic and often sad, whether in Austria or Hungary or Rumania.

Otherwise, it must be admitted, the Danube is inferior to the Rhine. Rhine wines are famous and Danube wines are not. Already in the days of my youth the Rhine was crowded with endless trains of barges and tugs flying the flags of Switzerland, Germany, France and Holland; the Danube, by comparison, was deserted. For on the Rhine there was industry and wealth, and on the Danube there was poverty. The further East, the mightier grew the river, the poorer grew the people. But there was the 'Imperial Royal Privileged First Danube Steamship Company' which could boast not only the longest name of any Austrian enterprise and the emperor himself as its first shareholder, but also a few smart ships with comfortable sleeping accommodation; and travellers suffering from nervous strain could float down all the way from Passau through Vienna and Budapest to Giurgiu in Rumania, a soothing journey which took longer than the Atlantic crossing from Southampton to New York without making any demands on the seaworthiness of the passengers.

In sight of Vienna the hills on both banks recede and the plain opens its arms wide. 'In sight of Vienna.' The Danube, in fact, gets no nearer than that to the 'Danube Town' and uninformed visitors may be disappointed to find that Vienna is not on the Danube as London is on the Thames and Paris on the Seine or Rome on the Tiber. One had to travel by tram or hansom cab some two miles North from the town through a belt of woods and thickets, part fen land, part grove, part coppice where in early March a profusion of snowdrops and scented violets announced the coming of spring and floods. But although the Danube makes no effort to greet the visitor to Vienna, the visitor would make the effort to greet the Danube because of Johann Strauss's waltz hymn to 'the beautiful blue Danube', only to be disappointed again. For the Danube is not beautiful in the ordinary sense and it is not blue at any time of day or year. But it is majestic, gigantic, and the driving force of its current is almost frightening. Only Herculean swimmers or oarsmen could venture out into the stream to be swept away at an alarming pace. But the Viennese made the giant smile—in sight of Vienna.

Onward the Danube rolls into the plain. With the hills, Europe recedes. No longer disciplined by mountains its bed becomes wider and the current slackens. Cormorants and herons populate the water and storks walk stiffly on the banks. Twenty miles East of Vienna a small river joins the Danube on the right bank, the Leitha, small in size but large in significance. For until the 'Collapse' it marked the border between Austria and Hungary. One used to speak of 'Cis-Leithania' or Austria, and 'Trans-Leithania' or Hungary, as the Romans spoke of

'Cis-Alpine' and 'Trans-Alpine' Gaul, so distinguishing between Europe and Not-Quite-Europe. Up to the West bank of the Leitha people spoke German, the Bavaro-Austrian variety of German, and called the Danube 'Donau'. On the other bank, hardly fifty yards away, they spoke Hungarian and called the Danube 'Duna'. Otherwise there was no real frontier there, no customs, no passports. The frontier indeed existed only for geographers, historians and patriots and not for ordinary mortals, and the trains of the 'Imperial Royal Eastern Railway' to and from Budapest did not bother to stop. And the Danube, too, passed the point with majestic indifference.

A few miles further to the East the Danube branches out into several arms forming two islands, the 'Large' and the 'Small' Schütt Islands. Centuries ago travellers on the river had to be on their guard and few passed the islands unharmed, for they were the haunt of a family of Hungarian highwaymen, the Esterházys, who caught and robbed the passing ships and so amassed a great fortune which, in more orderly times, made them thoroughly respectable princes with castles and palaces in the country, in Budapest and Vienna, lovers of the arts and Joseph Haydn's employers and patrons.

Further East still the Carpathian mountains from the North stretch a warning finger of hard rock towards the Danube and force it to turn sharply South, the only point where it allows itself to be deflected from its stubborn urge to the East. And soon it reaches Budapest, the capital of Hungary, but not of the Monarchy, which the river cuts in two or where, more precisely, it divides the old town of Buda from the new town of Pest. And past the capital the 'other side' of Europe unfolds, a steppe that could be anywhere in Asia, the 'Puszta', flat and featureless, with scattered villages and hamlets and draw wells, with grazing sheep and cattle and half-wild horses, the land of the 'csárda', the lonely thatched farmhouse; the 'csárdas', the fiery, stamping dance; of the 'csikos' or Hungarian-type cowboy, as perfect a horseman as his colleagues from Texas or Arizona; and of strange folksongs unknown in any other part of Europe. And the 'Duna' flows leisurely through the sunbaked country until the mountains gather round it again and send it gushing through the rapids of the Iron Gate where, as if in a sudden hurry, it left the Monarchy.

The Danube has a few hundred miles more to go before it finally tires and allows its waters to find their own way through vast mud flats and reed beds to the Black Sea, an unworthy goal, one might say, for such a mighty, much-sung, much-loved stream.

Rivers such as the Danube are not only picture-books. They are story-tellers, too. With all its 'wrong' direction the Danube was for Europe a river of destiny. It once guarded the Roman Empire. Not only Emperor Trajan left his mark at the Iron Gate. A few miles East of Vienna stands the Pagans' Gate, a huge archway in the midst of fields where ploughing peasants used to unearth Roman silver coins with the effigy of Emperor Marcus Aurelius who, in A.D. 180, died in the fortified camp called 'Vindobona', now Vienna.

Opening wide a back door into and out of Europe, the river later showed hosts of uninvited intruders the way. The Huns, the Avares, the Magyars or Hungarians, rode along its banks on their raids to the West. Later still crusaders sailed upon it on their way to and from the Holy Land and one of them, King Richard Cœur-de-Lion of England, was captured by a duke of Austria—not yet a Habsburg—and released only after payment of an extortionate ransom which ruined England's finances for many years. The Nibelungs also came down the Danube on their way to King Etzel and to their destruction; not Richard Wagner's treacherous pagan gods and cheated mortals, but their Christian cousins of the mediaeval epic.

Conditions then became more stable and life more secure. The Turks tried to break through, but Vienna held firm. When, in 1716, Lady Montagu came down the river in an 'Ulm Box', a kind of houseboat, she probably saw between Passau and Vienna the same sights, towns, villages, castles and abbeys as one could see at the beginning of this century although one of the most splendid Danube monasteries, Melk, was not yet finished.

However, one event above all others gave the Danube its historic significance: the arrival of the Habsburgs along its banks.

2

The House of Austria

Wondrous tales have been told about careers made in the New World by errand boys rising to become multi-millionaires. But all the stories of the Carnegies, Fords and Vanderbilts pale into insignificance when compared with the career of the Swiss family of the Habsburgs. A Swiss family: not far from the town of Aarau in North-West Switzerland a village and a small but well-preserved castle are still called Habsburg. That is their ancestral home and cradle.

Schoolchildren all over the old Monarchy were taught that in 1273 the German Electors chose an unimportant, virtually unknown Count Rudolf of Habsburg to be their king, and emperor of the Holy Roman Empire, not because of his merits or his power, but because his very insignificance would prevent him from interfering with their own dubious designs. And there, so we were told, they made a grave mistake. The story made good reading, but it was not quite true. The Habsburgs certainly did not belong among the most powerful families but neither were they entirely insignificant. They owned land from the Rhine near Basel down to Lucerne on the lake of that name. Rudolf's father, Count Albrecht, with enterprise and foresight had opened up the Gotthard Pass by building a mule track across the mountains from the Reuss to the Ticino valley. This soon became the most direct and most frequented highway from Central Europe to Italy and the toll exacted by their bailiffs swelled the Habsburg treasury. Moreover, the Habsburgs were kinsmen of the much wealthier counts of Kyburg and Count Rudolf in due course inherited the Kyburg lands from the lake of Constance to the neighbourhood of Zürich, together with the Kyburg which, like the Habsburg, still adorns the landscape. Even so, the election of Count Rudolf was a stroke of luck.

Austrian schoolchildren also had to learn a poem to be recited on appropriate occasions which praised the ancestral castle of Habsburg for the absence of wall and moat. The Habsburgs, it said, were such kindly people that they had no enemies and did not need the crude protection of stone and mortar for their safety. Count Rudolf was made to say to a visiting bishop: 'My protection are the men and women of my lands.' And this again was not quite true. The Habsburgs had their most determined and most dangerous enemies *within* their own borders, for the Gotthard tolls brought them into conflict with the Swiss, a conflict which began with the legend of William Tell and the foundation of the Swiss Confederation and ended nearly a hundred years later with the defeat and death of a Habsburg duke at the hands of Swiss peasants and with the loss of almost all their Swiss possessions.

However, by that time the Habsburgs were well compensated elsewhere. For King Rudolf, after his coronation, resolutely grasped the reins of government. Germany after twenty-three years without a king was in great disorder. As there was no ruler in Austria either, the King of Bohemia, whom we will meet again, occupied Austria and installed himself in Vienna, the first champion and victor of the gravitational force of the Danube Basin. It was King Rudolf's first duty to reconquer the stolen lands and he did. He defeated and killed the Bohemian king—but instead of returning the Austrian lands to the 'Reich' he kept them for himself and his house. Austrian historians regard the day of the Battle of Dürnkrut, August 26, 1278, as the birthday of the most enduring, most numerous and most powerful dynasty in Europe. Without losing any time King Rudolf set in train the phenomenal expansion of Habsburg power. He did not even trouble to make the traditional journey to Rome to receive from the Pope the crown of the Holy Roman Empire, which earned him Dante's sneer of 'the shopkeeper king'.

Conspicuous by little more than a protruding lower jaw, the 'Habsburg lip', which stayed with them for nearly five hundred years, sometimes assuming grotesque proportions as may be seen in the portraits of their court painter Velasquez in the seventeenth century, the Habsburgs' consistency replaced more distinguished, but less reliable qualities. None of them was a great warrior and none believed in conquests with sword and lance. It did not mean that they were modest and satisfied with what they already possessed. But they had subtler means of aggrandizement—sons and daughters who were cheaper and safer than armies and armour. Their fertility was indeed exceptional. Rudolf I had eleven children, his son Albrecht thirteen; and later fifteen, sixteen and even eighteen children, all legitimate, were no exception. In the eighteenth century Empress Maria Theresa wrote to one of her daughters: 'In this respect I am insatiable. One cannot have enough of them.' And she had sixteen children. With their nursery so well stocked the archhouse could dominate and survive all other ruling houses. And it did. Within a hundred years the Habsburgs acquired all the lands which until 1918 formed the German- and Italian-speaking parts of their future empire, from the Leitha in the East to the Swiss border in the West, from the Danube in the North to the Adriatic in the South. No sword had been drawn, no blood had been shed. It was all achieved by marriage contracts and providence was seemingly on the side of the Habsburgs.

But the crowning success of their match-making was still to come. Almost exactly two hundred years after the battle which started the Habsburgs on their way to greatness, Archduke, later Emperor, Maximilian I—'the last knight', poet and Albrecht Dürer's patron—married the only daughter of Charles Hardi, Duke of Burgundy. In the same year, the duke—by contrast, too fond of wars—was killed in battle and the Habsburgs found themselves in Flanders, in Bruges and Ghent, in Antwerp and Brussels, in the richest country in Europe, and at the most refined and extravagant court. This happy result encouraged Maximilian to a bold and risky step: he married his son Philip to 'mad' Joan, the only daughter of the 'Catholic Kings' of united Spain, Ferdinand and Isabella. After their death the Habsburg double-eagle was embossed on the gates of Toledo and the black and yellow banner was hoisted in the Iberian peninsula, in Naples and Sicily and Milan, in Cuba, Mexico, Chile and Peru. The kingdoms of Bohemia and Hungary soon joined the empire and Maximilian's grandson, Charles Quint, ruled a good third of the then known world. The misdeeds of the Conquistadores in the New World apart, still no shot had been fired, no battle fought. A Habsburg court poet could sum

it up in a hexameter: 'Bella gerant alii, tu felix Austria nube.'
'Wars may be waged by others, you, happy Austria, marry.'
Happy Austria! The Habsburgs liked to forget their Swiss origin
but they remained faithful to the country where their star had
first risen and even as kings of Castile and Leon and of the
'Country in the Oceanic Sea', they called themselves 'The
House of Austria'—'La Casa d'Austria'.

Their peaceful progress saved innumerable lives and spared
many countries much tribulation. It should have earned the
Habsburgs, if not the admiration, at least the gratitude of contemporaries and of posterity. Unfortunately the conqueror cuts
a better figure in history than the schemer, and the envy they
aroused seemed more legitimate than their bloodless acquisi-
tions.

Poor Charles Quint, the mightiest ruler since Alexander the
Great and Emperor Augustus, did not enjoy his power and his
greatness. Protestantism in Germany forced him into war. He
had to defend Catholicism even against the Pope and Rome was
sacked in his name, the most heinous crime in all history, it was
said. An old and disillusioned man at 55, he abdicated and left
his son Philip to rule the Western, and his brother the Eastern,
empire. The Habsburgs had reached the very summit; they
could climb no higher.

Philip once more tried the old Habsburg game with England
as the target. But Mary Tudor died and the Armada was
destroyed. It was the turning point in Habsburg's fortunes.

Reformation and revolution, the Turks, the Thirty Years
War, the French, the whole world seemed to conspire to break
the arch-house. Under the stresses of a new era the old fertility
flagged. A hundred years after Philip's death only one Habsburg
was left in Spain and when he died all the Spanish lands in
Europe and overseas except the Netherlands were lost to the
French Bourbons. Two brothers remained in Austria, one of
whom died unexpectedly of smallpox and the other, Charles VI,
had no son. The male line of the old house was extinct. With
Maria Theresa, Charles's daughter, married to Duke Francis of
Lorraine, the renovated and redecorated house of Habsburg-
Lorraine began its rule. Dreams of world empire were at an end
and the Habsburgs had to turn to the East where Hungary at
long last had been liberated from the Turks.

Strangely enough, Maria Theresa no longer had the traditional Habsburg appetite for more land. When, in the first partition of Poland, the dukedom of Halics—Galicia—was allotted to Austria, she wrote under the document: 'Placet, because so many learned and honest men approve of it. But when I shall be long dead, it will be seen what happens when everything is violated which up to now has been held to be sacred and just.' No Habsburg before her would have had such qualms if a country had been given to him.

Instead of venturing into world politics Maria Theresa applied her motherly care to her people, to her family, to her residence. It was, compared with the past, an unusually narrow circle of activities, but quite rewarding for a woman of no more than good sense. She set up a 'Commission of Morals' which, in the 'permissive' age of the Rococo, watched over high society and common people alike. To her sixteen children she issued 'rules of conduct' with the heading: 'To be read once every month'; she had the summer palace of Schönbrunn near Vienna with its 'Gloriette' rebuilt by Italian architects as it stands today; her physician Gerhard van Swieten, a native of still Austrian Flanders, founded the famous Viennese medical school. It was all small-scale and eminently useful and earned her a large monument in Vienna, the first Habsburg to be so honoured.

Maria Theresa's son Joseph II, a German emperor again, was the 'enlightened', absolute monarch after the fashion of the time, a rash reformer who commanded his peoples to be happy or be damned. But he was no less popular than his mother for his un-Habsburg delight in mixing with ordinary people and for his sense of duty rather than dignity. He lived to see the beginning of the French Revolution and when asked what he would do if his sister Marie Antoinette, Queen of France, was guillotined he replied brusquely: 'The state has no sister'. And he, too, was given a monument in one of Vienna's most beautiful squares, an equestrian statue representing him as a Roman 'imperator', which strangely misses his character. But there is no doubt that, under him, the arch-house and the people came closer together.

Maria Theresa's grandson, Emperor Franz, in Austria the first, in Germany the second of that name, saw the fateful nine-

teenth century in. He is often regarded as the true grave-digger
of the Monarchy. He had to face Napoleon and was no match
for him. He fought him without enthusiasm—no Habsburg ever
fought with enthusiasm—and was equally suspicious of French
liberté as of Prussian nationalism. Nor did he have the cool
composure of the British. Disgusted with the German princes
who joined Napoleon, he threw away the German imperial
crown which was never to sit on a Habsburg head again and
called himself more modestly 'Emperor of Austria'. And in the
wars Austria was badly mauled. It lost half its territory.
Although after a series of defeats the Austrian army had the
distinction of halting Napoleon in the Battle of Aspern in 1809,
it suffered the crushing defeat of Wagram only six weeks later.
Adding insult to injury, Franz's only daughter had to marry the
upstart from Corsica.

Four years later, in 1813, Austria played a decisive part in
the victory at Leipzig. It had the largest army in the field,
an Austrian field-marshal with an Austrian chief of staff in
command of the allied armies, but the honours went to Prussia
and Russia. However, Vienna with its palaces and pleasure
grounds which had twice welcomed Napoleon was the scene of
the great Congress, the largest assembly ever of emperors, kings,
princes, ambassadors, adventurers and courtisans. The imperial
city became both famous and notorious and the Austrians
quickly forgot the troubles of the preceding years.

When the Congress dispersed, somewhat hurriedly and discon-
certingly, Emperor Franz settled down to his task of turning the
clock back to the days when citizens were subjects and willingly
believed in the greater wisdom of their rulers. All the unwanted
ideas left behind by the Great Revolution and Napoleon were
to be eradicated. There were, there still are and, I suspect, there
always will be two ways of countering unwelcome new ideas:
better and newer ideas—or the police. Better ideas are usually
difficult to come by, but there has never been a régime, however atrocious or absurd, which has not found a loyal police,
one of the more discouraging features of human society.
Emperor Franz, like most of his colleagues on European thrones,
chose the police. An army of spies went to work and the chiefs of
police in every town wrote voluminous reports about suspicious
persons. A rigid censorship was clamped down on writers and

writings, on the theatre and on the press. Nobody was shot or beheaded, but some were sent to prison. One would have thought that it was an unhappy time but, strangely enough, it was not. The régime was absurd rather than atrocious and the Viennese in particular laughed at the gaucheries of the police and at the censor when he passed Shakespeare's *Macbeth* 'on condition that the soldiers do not wear Austrian uniform'. For the Viennese those were the good old days of the 'Biedermeier' or bourgeois affluence, of nicely designed and inlaid furniture and pretty fashions for men and women, the carefree 'fried chicken days' when the waltz was born, a glorious child of unknown parentage. And the emperor, who spoke Viennese like a coachman, was to everybody 'the good Emperor Franz'.

But the morale of the arch-house sagged ominously. A younger brother of the emperor, Archduke Johann, married not simply a commoner, which had happened before when the commoner was a fabulously rich lady. Archduke Johann married a postmaster's daughter and was proud of it. He drank beer and played skittles with the peasants in a Styrian village, was a farmer, and created a fashion by introducing the grey suit with green lapels, black hat with green band and chamois beard which are still an almost national costume in Styria and Upper Austria, in Vienna, Salzburg and Munich.

However, the good Emperor Franz could not turn the clock back as far as he had hoped. With his dim-witted son, Ferdinand, the good old days came to an end. Unrest spread from Germany and Italy, not to mention France, and on March 13, 1848 the barricades went up in Vienna and many other cities in Austria, revolution broke out in Hungary, and war in Lombardy. 'What do they want?', the emperor asked his first minister when a howling mob besieged the Hofburg. 'Liberty, Sir', Prince Metternich replied. 'Why don't you give it to them?' the emperor said. It earned him the nickname 'the Benevolent', but for the family council of archdukes and archduchesses it was the last straw and he was told to abdicate; which he did with a smile of relief, retiring to the empty castle in Prague. 'I could have done equally well', he said with a sly twinkle after the misfortunes of 1859 and 1866.

Ferdinand's eighteen-year-old nephew Franz Joseph, the first and last, was called upon to rescue the empire. An army of

Croats subdued Vienna, old Field-Marshal Radetzky, former chief of staff at Leipzig in 1813, routed the Piedmontese in Lombardy, a Russian corps beat the Hungarian rebels, and the Monarchy was saved once more. But even the most optimistic observer had to admit that fate itself had lost its respect for the arch-house. As a soldier Franz Joseph was a disaster, in politics he was unlucky, his private life was a succession of tragedies.

Only once, in 1859, he assumed command of the armed forces and was defeated by the allied French and Piedmontese at Solferino. Milan and Lombardy were lost.

Seven years later, in 1866, he left strategy to professional soldiers and sat in a room at the Northern Railway Station in Vienna where a direct telegraph line to headquarters in Bohemia had been installed. There he was the first to hear the news of the débâcle at Königgrätz (or Sadowa, as the French called it). In its own way that war was typically Austrian. It was a war on two fronts, against the Prussians in Bohemia and the Italians in Lombardy. The war against the Prussians was, for Franz Joseph, as unpopular as the war against the Italians was popular. An archduke was given the easier command in the South, a general who had served all his life in Italy and knew every village and footpath there was sent to the North. 'I told them that in the Northern theatre I am an ass', he wrote despairingly to his wife before the war even started. In the South the archduke covered himself with glory, routing the Italians on the same battlefields where Field-Marshal Radetzky had defeated them before; while the hapless general was beaten by the Prussians, thus effectively cancelling out the Italian victory. The emperor hastened to offer armistice terms and Bismarck, for both the Prussians and the Italians, hastened to accept them. The city and province of Venice, the last Austrian possession in Upper Italy, were to be handed over to the new kingdom of Italy. But in the confusion of defeat and victory somebody forgot to advise the Austrian admiral in Pola. Austria, let it be remembered, had a navy and a naval base in the Adriatic, a fact which the emperor was apt to forget. The Habsburgs came from the mountains and were not at home at sea. Franz Joseph had in his wardrobe the colonel's uniform of every one of his hundred-odd infantry, cavalry and artillery

23

regiments but no admiral's outfit. So, believing that the war was still to be won and hearing that the Italian fleet had put to sea, the Austrian admiral set sail and, nearly three weeks after the war had been lost, fell upon the Italians and destroyed their fleet, battleships, cruisers, 'avviso' boats and all. This posthumous 'victory' did the humiliated empire a power of good. It was finally expelled from the German federation which, five years later, became the German Reich under Prussian leadership, with the king of Prussia assuming the style and dignity of emperor or 'Kaiser' of Germany.

Austria was no longer a great power. Henceforth, world events gave her a wide berth, thinking perhaps: 'Elle est brisée, n'y touchez pas.' Other powers, Britain, France, Germany, even Italy scrambled for colonies overseas, while an Austrian Arctic expedition discovered an uncharted island off Novaja Zemlja, called it 'Franz Josephs Land' and hoisted the black and yellow flag among seals and polar bears, a colony at last, inexpensive and unprofitable.

The emperor could now apply himself to Austria's internal, interminable troubles. Hungarians, Czechs, Italians, socialists and democrats clamoured for independence, federalization, democratization, constitution. Cabinets came and went, twenty-one in forty-three years, each one undoing what its predecessors had done. Parliament was established, with two dozen parties aptly called 'fractions', most if not all of them in opposition not only to the government but to each other, often for opposition's sake. 'I do not know the government's intentions,' one opposition member once cried, 'but I disapprove of them.' The emperor was indeed his own 'loyal' opposition, opposed to parliament, democracy, and franchise. Opposition in parliament usually ended in obstruction of various degrees. An opposition member would speak for twenty-four hours sustained by his friends with sandwiches and glasses of water; or at the next stage members would throw inkpots at each other; or, in the last resort, they would walk out. The emperor would then restore the dignity of the temple on the Ringstrasse in Vienna by sending all the parliamentarians home on unspecified leave and would put his shoulder harder against the door in an attempt to keep the new era out of his realm.

His peoples could have been cross with him had fate not

taken the whip out of their hands. There was no unhappier man in all his lands than he.

First his brother Maximilian, in a farce with a tragic ending, allowed himself to be made emperor of Mexico only to be executed by a firing squad in Queretaro. It was said that the old Mexican gods had taken belated revenge for the brutalities perpetrated three hundred years earlier by Pizarro and his men in Habsburg's name.

Then Franz Joseph's only son, Crown Prince Rudolf, first associated with democrats and other suspect people and then threw away his life in the much-described, over-dramatized and frequently-filmed tragedy of Mayerling.

A few years later the emperor's beautiful but somewhat way-ward wife, Empress Elizabeth, was stabbed to death in Geneva by an anarchist who had no personal grudge against her or the emperor.

Franz Joseph's nephew and, after the crown prince's death, heir to the throne married a lady below his rank and so dis-qualified his sons from the succession. This archduke, Franz Ferdinand, made the ominous observation that the emperor's crown was a martyr's crown which should not be coveted by anyone who was not singled out by destiny. And he, too, was murdered, the first Habsburg ever to be assassinated for political reasons; and, it was said afterwards, unjustly. The Slavs in the Monarchy suspected him of being a German nationalist for they had seen him too often in the company of Kaiser Wilhelm. But historians insisted that he would have given home rule to the Slavs had he been allowed the oppor-tunity.

The arch-house was in grave disarray and the end was loom-ing large.

But Franz Joseph bore it all with singular dignity. Chained to his throne by a blind sense of duty, he worked doggedly day in day out through masses of papers with little time and less inclination to think. In Schönbrunn, which he preferred to the Hofburg, his private rooms could have been any caretaker's home; an iron bedstead, no running water, no personal com-fort. Every morning at five o'clock, by when the emperor was already fully dressed and had heard morning mass, the editor of a moderately progressive paper had to appear before him and report on the political situation. The summer was spent in the 'Kaiser Villa' in Bad Ischl in the Upper Austrian Alps where all the jokers of the Monarchy met, the librettists and composers of the Viennese operettas, to sell or buy new ideas, where contracts worth hundreds of thousands were drawn or torn up. But the 'Kaiser Villa' stood apart and only a highly respectable actress of the Hofburg Theatre kept the lonely man company without any hint of anything unseemly between them. Yet when a whisper went round she broke off the friendship and thereafter the emperor was to be seen only in the company of two other old gentlemen, his aide-de-camp Count Paar and his physician Dr Kerzl.

No wonder that even the noisiest opponents of his policies thought with compassion and even affection of the emperor whom they knew only as an old, unhappy man. And as long as he lived no Austrian of whatever nationality or political belief could seriously imagine that one day the national anthem would be untrue and Austria's destinies would no longer be united with Habsburg's throne.

3

Austria felix!

After all the disasters which in quick succession had befallen their country and their ruler, one might have expected to find the Austrians—and particularly the Viennese—dejected and dispirited. But nothing would have been further from the truth. The Austrians never fancied the brutality of worldly power nor the vulgarity of great worldly riches, an unambitious people aiming no higher than the special Austrian or Viennese 'Gemütlichkeit'. The word is not German but Austrian and cannot be translated into any other language, for the object does not exist anywhere else. It is a compound of cosiness, snugness, conviviality, something relaxed and atmospheric rather than tangible, felt rather than defined. One cannot produce it; it produces itself. It would be spoilt by want no less than by wealth. A good deal of the charm of Vienna and the Viennese lies in this 'Gemütlichkeit' which emerged undimmed from all the adversities of those twilight years. Nothing could illustrate it more convincingly than the music which at that time flooded out of Vienna and set the whole world dancing, the music of Johann Strauss, Suppé, Zeller, Ziehrer. Viennese music may have been 'greater' in the past, but it had never been happier or sweeter.

Moreover, the economy—like many other things—was more robust and could not easily be shaken by lost wars and lost provinces. Neither Austria in 1866 nor France in 1871 were thrown into disarray. The wars were short, battlefields and destruction were limited to a few square miles, the gold-based currencies were as stable as rocks and the world was wide open for anyone who wished to look for better chances abroad. Few Austrians, however, availed themselves of such opportunity. The younger sons of Czech, Hungarian or Polish peasants emigrated to the United States, for they had few expectations at home where only the eldest son could inherit his father's house and holding. But when a member of the upper or middle classes went to live abroad, eyebrows were raised and rumours of debts, girls, or the police went round. It simply was not done because there was no good reason to do it.

So for people with limited ambitions there were no grounds for despondency. After all, Austria was still a large country of great variety. There was Southern Tyrol, a perfect paradise. The central chain of the Alps divides the Danube from the Po, the Black Sea from the blue Adriatic, the bad weather from the good. There were the fantastic shapes of the Dolomites where edelweiss grow in the fields like daisies and the sunset paints the yellow rocks pink and purple. There were Misurina and Cortina, places of extravagant beauty, Bozen and Meran where the famous 'Calville' apples grew and muscatel grapes and people spoke the guttural Tyrolese German and ate Tyrolese dumplings, Arco with the northernmost olive groves, and Lake Garda, the bluest of all the blue lakes of the Southern Alps, where the people spoke Italian.

There was also the Adriatic, equally blue and warm, the beaches of Grado, the bay of Trieste with the fairy castle of Miramar and the white-painted ships of the 'Triestiner Lloyd' and the 'Cosulich Line' which would take one South along the enchanted coast and islands of Dalmatia to Spalato—not yet Split—with Diocletian's palace, to Ragusa—not yet Dubrovnik, and to the fjord of Cattaro—not yet Kotor, into another world, into the Orient with its mosques and minarets.

Admittedly, there were other and less attractive provinces; Galicia in the North-East, flat and bare, choking in dust in summer, drowning in mud in autumn and spring, buried under huge snowdrifts in winter, with grandiloquent churches and palaces in the towns and poor huts in the villages, with ghettoes of orthodox Jews in their 'kaftans' and round hats, and garrisons and fortresses facing the black and white posts along the Russian border. There were the wild peaks and ravines of the Carpathian mountains and the dark forests of Bukovina and Slavonia where wolves and brown bears still roamed.

All this was Austria as I remember it. However strange the habits and incomprehensible the language of the people, one felt at home. For everywhere one could see the same uniforms of the army and the 'gendarmerie' or country police, of railway-men and postmen. Everywhere one found the same black and yellow letter-boxes designed like little renaissance palaces, the same dirty little post offices selling the same stamps with the emperor's unmistakable effigy, and the same dirty little shops called 'Tabak Trafik' where one bought the articles of the state monopoly, cigars, cigarettes and tobacco of the imperial-royal 'Tabak Regie'; salt, the mining and distribution of which was reserved to the state; and tickets for the 'lotto', the little man's lottery run by the state where road-sweepers and housemaids could put a 'kreuzer' or penny on a number of which they had dreamt and could win a 'gulden' or two shillings if, after the draw, the number was chalked up on the blackboard of the 'Trafik'. But law and self-respect forbade the 'Trafikant' to sell anything else such as sweets or stationery. Everywhere there was the same indisciplined order somnambulating between regimentation and chaos which was the hallmark of Austrian administration.

An Englishman would find it objectionable if he was required to register with the police and keep the police informed of his whereabouts. But this is exactly what Austrians had to do. Wherever they lived, whenever they changed their address, they had to tell the police. The uninformed foreigner might have thought that Austria was a police state, but it was not. As long as the citizen told the police, he could go where and when he wanted both in the Monarchy or abroad. Indeed, those were the legendary days when no passport was needed and exchange controls were unknown. The Western Hemisphere apart, there were only a few ill-reputed countries which required passports and visas such as Russia, Turkey or Spain. But the police wanted to know and were curious for the traveller's own sake. Announcements such as are heard today on the radio: 'Would so-and-so last heard of three years ago . . .' were quite unthink-able. The police always knew where to find their wandering sheep and if they did not know, it was the fault of the wanderer and he was fined. But the curiosity of the police did not stop at his address. They wanted to know the age, birthplace, profession and religion of every householder and of all those who lived with him. No apparent use was made of all this information but it must have given the authorities the feeling that they were governing the country.

Twenty years after the foundation of the 'Société des Bains de Mer' in Monte Carlo, resorts began to be developed in Austria where people with time and money could go without pretext of particular ailments. Hotels arose in Bad Ischl, Meran, Abbazia and Laurana, not casinos where one could make a fortune or lose it overnight and shoot oneself, but respectable 'Kur Hotels', 'Kur Promenades', 'Kur Theatres' and 'Kur Concerts' without any other cure than mountains, sea and sunshine. Mother, who every year in February developed a nasty cough, was always whisked away to Meran where the trees were already in full blossom and her catarrh vanished miraculously in twenty-four hours. None of these places were of the luxury standard of the Côte d'Azur but it was all solid and 'gemütlich' without any extravagance.

But nothing in Austria was extravagant, neither wealth nor poverty, neither work nor pleasure. There was plenty of land but little of it was wasted on sports or games. There were no golf courses, no football grounds, and only half a dozen racecourses in the whole Monarchy. Only the uppermost classes cared for horse-racing and the turf could not compete with the lotto. While such unusual professions as tight-rope walkers or lion-tamers were barely legitimate, a professional sportsman would have been regarded as a wrongdoer. I remember flying on a Saturday afternoon from the Continent into Northolt airport not long after the Second World War when the little DC-3 planes flew no higher than 1,000 feet. From Dover to Harrow there were dozens of village greens dotted with the white figures of cricketers. No such sight could have been seen in Austria where the lordly game was and still is unknown.

In cafés and inns of the the North, in 'osterias' in the South, men played harmless and inexpensive card games the names of which I still remember, though not the rules: 'tarock', 'mariage', 'preference'. By order of the police, tables and benches in the 'osterias' had to be of stone because in still older days the players had the uncomfortable habit of ramming their knives into the wooden furniture so as to have them handy in case of disagreements. Skittles in the North were matched by 'boccia' in the South, which was even more harmless and less expensive and equally entertaining. In the open fields of the North there were plenty of partridges and hares and in the shooting season butchers in the towns displayed whole strings of them. But in the South, Italian peasants went shooting singing birds. There was an 'Animal Protection Society' in Vienna but it was powerless when confronted with the unquenchable passion of the Italians in the Southern provinces (and all over Northern Italy) for 'uzei con polenta', roast larks, finches, thrushes accompanied by that maize pudding which, as 'pulmentum', had already served Roman legionaries as staple food and iron ration.

I do not pretend to remember much about the womenfolk. The state, which assumed full responsibility for the education of boys, allowed girls only the barest minimum of it. Their schooling ended at the age of fourteen and thereafter they had to prepare themselves for the more tangible requirements of their future life. They seemed quite contented and there were no suffragettes. Ladies of the middle classes such as my mother, aunts and older cousins had, apart from their normal chores, one hobby or even passion which was embroidery. Whenever and wherever ladies met they embroidered something. Every tablecloth, handkerchief, napkin, towel, pillow case and shirt had mother's self-made embroidered monogram; curtains and bedspreads were made at home and embroidered. On the walls of the nursery hung few pictures, but squares of linen with embroidered children catching embroidered butterflies, and useful ditties such as: 'Never till tomorrow delay the work that you can do today.' And similar admonitions in the kitchen reminded the cook: 'With coal good cooks economize, for coal is dear and cooks are wise.' Doctors thought that embroidering was a healthy occupation and recommended it even to males of a nervous disposition. But with all her endless embroidering, mother was very nervous and, like most ladies of the time, suffered from migraine.

The picture of Austrian society would be incomplete without a mention of the Austrian nobility which abroad was often taken as truly representative of true Austrianism. What was called 'bagatelle nobility' did not count for much: generals, high civil servants, meritorious industrialists who received a low grade title. True nobility had to be old and their merits long forgotten. This blue-blooded nobility was numerous and scattered through all the provinces. And it was all landed. Some families were very wealthy and others less so. They scorned industry or commerce or, in general, common work and if they needed a supplementary income they went into the army, preferably the 'Black Dragoons', for they were good horsemen, or into the diplomatic service, for they spoke French, wore the gold-braided uniform of the 'corps diplomatique' with incomparable grace and found the doors of high society in every country open; and that was then a most important part of a diplomat's mission. Few of them were highly educated and one did not meet them often at universities. But they had exquisite manners and natural charm, they did not wear monocles and click their heels like Prussian 'junkers' (clicking of heels was not the fashion in Austria), and their unawareness of ordinary problems made them lovable and funny. They were popular, for they were friendly and unpolitical and villagers were proud of 'their' count on whose estate they lived. Father's father, an upholsterer in a Moravian village and already an old man when I was a little boy, was the friend and adviser of the 'local' Count Mensdorff-Pouilly, an old man like himself. I remember grandfather taking off his hat whenever we passed the 'Schloss' or mansion for, he said, the 'Herr Graf' might be looking out of a window.

4

An Army for Peace

Wherever one went in the old Monarchy, the army was much in evidence. Those were still the days when 'battle dress' was unknown and soldiers were not meant to disappear into the crowd or the landscape, but to stand out and be conspicuous. A superficial observer could have jumped to the wrong conclusion that Austria was a highly militarized and militaristic country. It was true that every able-bodied young man of twenty-one had to serve for three years; and in a country of some fifty million this produced a standing army of a few hundred thousand. For a country which was rated as poor this seemed an extravagant luxury, particularly since what enemies there were were inside the country and, therefore, inside the army. Soldiers from general down to private had to wear uniform and side-arm, sabre or bayonet, on all occasions, on and off duty, in barracks and on leave, in church, theatre, café or restaurant. And so wherever people congregated there were soldiers and uniforms.

But while it was an army on the cheap, the strange thing was that it did not look cheap. The private received three pennies a day in cash, enough to take his girl out for a dance and a glass of beer on Sunday and to buy the small, thin cigarettes which were known as 'narrow-gauges', a packet of twenty for a penny. Beyond this he was well clothed, well fed and, in the circumstances, well housed. Indeed, if he was a peasant boy as most of them were, he lived in comparative luxury. Professional officers had to have private means, at least at the beginning of their career, for they had to observe certain standards, were not admitted to cheap seats in theatres and concert halls, were not to be seen in cheap cafés or restaurants and could not afford all this out of their meagre pay. Before they married they had to

33

deposit a certain sum with the War Ministry as a guarantee that their wives and children would also observe the social standards laid down for the 'imperial and royal' officers' corps. Therefore, the officer in debt and plagued by his creditors was a popular comic character on the stage. But sometimes more sinister stories were told of a captain who poisoned a rich aunt or of a colonel of the general staff who sold battle orders to the Russians and, in this world of cavaliers, was not subjected to the indignity of legal prosecution but was handed a loaded revolver which he understood as well as a mandarin in old China when sent a silken rope.

The army was smart and the uniforms were handsome; infantry no less than dragoons from Bohemia or Moravia, hussars from Hungary, Uhlans from Galicia and even the 'genie corps', sappers and pioneers. But smartness had nothing to do with efficiency. It was smartness for its own sake, so much so that the Viennese after the First World War regretfully said: 'We had the smartest army in the world—and have wasted it on a war.'

In fact, the thought that the ultimate purpose of any army was war would not have occurred to anyone. In sharp contrast to the German ally there was an air of apology about the Austrian army which prevented it from taking itself too seriously. Its institutions were the subject of much fun and ridicule and a comedy, *The Strategists' Hill*, amused audiences in all Austrian theatres and languages for many years. It paraded half-witted generals, amorous captains and clever privates. Even an archduke made an appearance in a general's dress uniform with a general's green-plumed hat, mistaking the identities of everyone, and a Prussian colonel, very different from his jolly Austrian comrades, was made to say: 'I am really a nice fellow, but when on duty I am a beast—and I am always on duty.' In 1909 Emmerich Kalmán's operetta *Autumn Manœuvres* owed its great success last but not least to the fun it poked at the army and few listeners would have disagreed with the budding officer when he sang: 'If I am sweating in the heat as if in a Turkish bath, pray, what good is it to the fatherland?'

However, the authorities, and many fathers, believed that the army served a useful purpose. The uniform was one of the few, and in some parts of the country the only, thing the eleven nations of the Monarchy had in common. Even the most out-spoken rebels had a soft spot for 'the emperor's coat' and believed that the three years in the service were a good educa-tion. Peasant boys from every corner of the Monarchy had to learn a few words of German, for German was the 'service' language; they were made to be punctual, brush their clothes and polish their boots. Life in the army sharpened their wit rather than deadening their sense of humour and the evasion of unpleasant duties was a sport practised by all ranks. I remember the lieutenant who gave us recruits our first instructions when the Great War broke out. With a broad smile he told us: 'Whenever there is a call for volunteers, step aside and let the volunteers come forward.'

However, the Austrian army had its own particular glory: its bands and bugle calls. Austrian bands had neither the pro-vocative sound of French or Italian bands nor the dull square-ness of Prussian military music. The marches had a happy lilt like the 'Radetzky March', the signature tune of the Austrian army, or were humorous, like the 'Entry of the Gladiators'. The army bands were the breeding ground of the famous light music which came from Vienna. Suppé, Ziehrer, Komzák, Lehár, Viennese, Hungarians, Czechs and Italians, they were all at one time or another 'Militärkapellmeister' as they were rather modestly called, and many a trumpeter or horn player in the Vienna Philharmonic Orchestra had served his apprentice-ship in an army band. And the bugle calls! I believe they were the most musical bugle calls of any army in the world; the 'Infantry March', the rhythm of which was so nicely laid out that a marching battalion with a bugle to each company marched to a perfect four-part canon; the 'Cavalry March', which was like a sketch of galloping horses, the 'Retraite'—many French terms had stayed in the Austrian service manual called 'règlement'—the call which summoned all soldiers to barracks at 9 p.m. and many a soldier to eternal rest as the 'Last Post'. If battles could have been won with bugle calls as in biblical times, Austria would never have lost a war.

5

The Imperial-Royal Capital
and Residence

Quite naturally, Austria and Austrianism were nowhere more concentrated and glorified than in Vienna, the 'Imperial-Royal Capital and Residence'.

Strange as it may seem, the Imperial-Royal city was the product of Habsburg's decline. As long as the Habsburgs prospered in the West, they did not care for the city far away on the Eastern fringe of their empire. Emperor Maximilian, the husband of Mary of Burgundy, preferred Innsbruck. Charles Quint, born in Ghent and to all intents and purposes a Spaniard, hardly knew it. At the end of the sixteenth century the Habsburg emperor resided in Prague. But when, in 1618, the Thirty Years War broke out, distant Vienna was the safest place. Compared with Brussels or Madrid, Vienna was then rather poor in appearance. There was no 'Maison du Roi', no Escorial, only the old castle of Habsburg's predecessors and St Stephen's Cathedral founded by a Bohemian king before the arrival of the first Habsburg. There were a few other old churches, but for the rest mainly walls, bastions and moats and gates; for since its foundations in the dim past Vienna had been a border fortress and even then, at the beginning of the seventeenth century, the Turks were barely a hundred miles away. Now, while the great war raged through all the provinces of Germany, though never within sight or sound of Vienna, the emperor installed himself in his capital and replaced the old castle by a new 'Hofburg'. He did it so thoroughly that nothing remains of the old structure which today is known only from old drawings. When the war was over Germany lay in ruins, but Vienna was unscathed. The imperial court remained and the nobility of the empire gathered round it, building its baroque palaces in the 'Inner Town'. And when, after the second and last siege, the Turks were driven out of Hungary, the empire expanded to the East and South-East and Vienna moved into the very centre. A few years later, after the loss of Spain, Vienna was the only residence worthy of the imperial presence and the Viennese had little reason to regret the eclipse of their rulers. More palaces, more churches were built and the growing splendour of the imperial court enveloped the whole city. In Empress Maria Theresa's time, in the middle of the eighteenth century, Vienna was not far behind Paris which had no more beautiful palaces than Prince Eugene's winter palace in town and his summer palace, the 'Belvedere', on the outskirts, no more imposing architecture than Charles' Church and Schönbrunn.

So, in the centre of the most colourful empire in Europe, the Viennese, Europe's 'Phaeacians'—as more ambitious people called them with an undertone of sarcasm—were well pleased with themselves and disinclined to take their temporary setbacks to heart. It was after the defeats of 1859 and 1866 that their city blossomed out just as it had done after the lost war of the Spanish succession. Vienna had long been huddled around St Stephen's which the Viennese to this day simply call 'St Stephen's Church' and neither 'Cathedral' nor 'Dom'. It was hemmed in by its fortifications like the ladies of the time in their corsets, while outside the walls the suburbs grew. The fortifications, once so useful, had become a danger rather than a protection. When, in 1805, Napoleon first marched on Vienna, the burgesses implored their emperor not to defend the city and expose it to destruction. And when, four years later, Napoleon came again and the Viennese made a gesture of defiance, a few shots convinced them that the preservation of their treasures was more important than a display of traditional bravery. It was bad enough that the shock from a shell bursting in his front garden caused old Joseph Haydn's death.

It was, therefore, a logical step that after the revolution of 1848 Emperor Franz Joseph ordered those irritating fortifications to be razed and the empty spaces of the 'glacis' to be filled with palaces and parks. And once again Vienna rose from the debris of defeat more beautiful than ever. One of the world's famous streets was so created, the Ringstrasse or Ring Road, not as grand as the Champs Elysées, not as haughty as Fifth Avenue, but exquisitely tasteful. It was perhaps a blessing in disguise that it was built in the shadow of misfortune. Berlin, rebuilt and embellished at the same time in the flush of victory, was an upstart by comparison.

Guide books will tell the reader all about the palatial buildings along the three and a half miles of the Ringstrasse; about the Court Opera being not the largest, but the most beautiful opera house in the world; about Parliament in the shape of a Greek temple guarded by Pallas Athene, the goddess of wisdom, behind whose back inside the temple so little wisdom was displayed; about the Imperial-Royal Hofburg Theatre, the most generously designed theatre in the style of Sansovino's 'Old Library' in Venice where marble staircases, 'promenoirs' and foyers hung with the portraits of all the famous actors and actresses of the German tongue take up more space than the theatre itself; about the Imperial-Royal Court Museums facing each other across Empress Maria Theresa's monument, one the Natural History Museum where the remains of the oldest inhabitants of the Danube Basin are exhibited, mammoth tusks and bones found in the subsoil of Vienna, the other the Art Gallery with the paintings of Habsburg court painters, of Titian, Dürer, Rubens, Velasquez, treasures from former Austrian provinces, from Florence, Venice, Parma, from the Netherlands and Spain, some of which had to be returned after the 'Collapse'.

In Berlin a Siegesallee, or Victory Avenue, was built where stone-faced general stood next to stone-faced general in absurd monotony. In Vienna no such avenue could have been conceived, not only because there were not enough victories but for reasons of good taste. However, there *is* a Heldenplatz, or Heroes' Square, which lies between the Hofburg, Parliament, the museums and the Hofburg Theatre. It is much more peaceful than the name would suggest for the wide space is planted with Spanish lilac which in May fills the whole neighbourhood with its sweet scent. There is no great assembly of heroes. Only two equestrian statues enjoy this elegant setting, one of Prince Eugene of Savoy, the other of Archduke Charles; and both have survived the 'Collapse'.

Prince Eugene certainly conforms to the popular image of a

hero. He was generalissimo of the Austrian armies in the war of the Spanish Succession and helped Marlborough to win the battles of Blenheim (in Austria called the battle of Höchstädt), Malplaquet and Oudenarde (which was particularly gratifying since Louis XIV had rejected his services). Thereafter he chased the Turks out of Hungary and Belgrade. But he was also a learned man, a patron of the arts and particularly of the two great Viennese baroque architects Fischer von Erlach who built his winter palace and Lucas von Hildebrandt who built his summer palace. That he was neither Viennese nor even Austrian by birth did not matter. He was both by mutual adoption.

The case of the other hero is more Austrian and more complicated. For the archduke on the rearing horse brandishing the colours of the Regiment Zach in its assault on the village cemetery of Aspern on a Whit Sunday, May 21, 1809, did not have a hero's career at all. He won the battle of Aspern and four weeks later lost the battle of Wagram only a few miles to the East, whereupon he was dismissed and never again given a command or any other office. He lived as a private citizen, married a Protestant lady, played the piano (as he had done before the victorious battle while his brother, the emperor, was on his knees praying for victory), had plenty of children and died leaving the cross of the Legion of Honour which Napoleon himself had sent to him, books on military matters, and a volume of aphorisms. None of these things should have singled him out for a monument in a 'Heroes' Square' and in such illustrious company as that of Prince Eugene. But there was an obvious injustice to be made good and the archduke was duly set up in bronze with his back resolutely turned on the effigy of his brother in the courtyard of the Hofburg.

'Heroes' Square' is not out of tune with the controlled elegance of the Ringstrasse, but the new Hofburg is, a large semi-circle of whitish stone with half columns and innumerable windows adjoining the older part of the imperial palace. Over-optimism clearly got the better of the planners and the empire could not wait until the palace was finished. Whenever I went to Vienna before the Great War, it seemed forever strangled in its scaffolding. The architect and his builders should have been in a hurry for there was little time to lose. But it was eventually left to the Republic to finish it and it took many years before the Republic knew what to do with it.

The Ringstrasse, like the Paris boulevard, was a place for the traveller without special interests. He could saunter along and look at the riders on the bridle path, or at the 'fiakers' and 'équipages' in the road, or sit down in one of the many cafés with chairs and tables on the pavement and be happy to enjoy it all. The discerning visitor would have sought the 'Inner Town' with its many baroque palaces in the narrow streets which made it difficult to appreciate their architecture, just as St Stephen's Square was really too narrow to see the church and its spire. Behind St Stephen's he would have found the house where Mozart wrote *The Marriage of Figaro* and he might even have strayed into the oldest part, into 'Greek Street' and 'Pretty Lantern Street' and into many a corner which had not changed since the days when Sultan Suleiman sent his Janissaries to storm the 'Bastei' which still stands opposite the New University with the Pasqualati House on top, one of the many houses where Beethoven lived.

Travellers coming from the East or South-East saw here the first—and vivid—flash of Europe, while those coming from the West who had been told that Austria was the other 'sick man' of Europe—the first being the Ottoman Empire—would have looked in vain for any symptom of malady.

6

The Imperial-Royal Railways

Every year about Easter time the family travelled from Prague to Vienna to see our relatives, mother's parents and father's brother, a bearded bachelor with a noisy and unfriendly dog growling behind a Chinese paravent of black silk with an embroidered silver dragon whose protruding red eyes frightened me each time I looked at it. But I loved my jolly grandfather, and my grandmother's home-made pastries, particularly one confection in the shape of sea-horses with ginger as the main ingredient which my mother for some reason never made.

We had, of course, travelled to Vienna by train and although the links between Prague and Vienna were sentimentally tenuous, there were two railway lines connecting the 'imperial' with the 'royal' city; the more direct 'Imperial-Royal Franz Joseph Railway' and the 'Imperial-Royal State Railway'. They were in fact both state railways for all the railways in Austria were nationalized.

Austrian railways were not quite as fastidious in their class-consciousness as the German railways, which had four classes; for the prominent, for the somebodys, for the everybodys and for the nobodys. Austrian railways had only three classes; a first class, upholstered, with three seats on each side of the compartment, reserved for the rich who could pay and for generals, high civil servants and members of parliament who did not have to pay; a second class, equally upholstered, with four seats on each side for middle-class people like ourselves; and a third class, with wooden benches and no standardised number of seats for the rest. There were not only compartments for smokers and non-smokers but also for ladies only, 'Damen Coupés'. It was all very orderly. I remember an old peasant getting into our second class compartment. When the conductor pointed out to

41

him that he was not only in the wrong compartment but in the wrong train, he spoke these unforgettably wise words: 'It is my duty to buy a ticket and your duty to get me home.' And refused to move.

In this pre-technological age the railway was the greatest sensation the world had to offer. Mother was nervous of losing father, children and luggage; father was outwardly calm but I suspect no less excited than I; and when the train hobbled along at the prescribed maximum speed of 60 kilometres, about 35 miles an hour, and the telegraph poles along the line executed a fantastic ballet, it seemed no less adventurous than flying today at 600 miles an hour. The new technical wonder of the motor-car had hardly penetrated as far East as the Danube Monarchy and the few who owned and drove these awkward, noisy contraptions were regarded as cranks. So the horse still held its own as man's most useful servant and the Austrian railways in particular could not do without its services. The reason for such collaboration of ancient and modern was thrift on the part of the railways, for they burned soft coal which was cheap and plentiful. Like every cheap thing it had a few snags. It made the engines, with their cone-shaped funnels, look at night like erupting volcanoes and responsible people worried about reckless progress were afraid that the imperial-royal railways would set the whole imperial-royal Monarchy on fire. Therefore railway lines carefully avoided every inhabited place they were meant to serve. Except in large towns where stone-built houses with tiled roofs gave better protection, railway stations stood forlornly in open country miles away from the destination the name of which was painted on their signboards. It was most inconvenient for travellers but a boon for owners of rickety char-à-bancs called 'Stellwagen', the last and impoverished descendants of the mail-coach which supplemented the service of the railway by transporting travellers and luggage to and from the station.

The soft coal inconvenienced travellers in yet another way. It blew clouds of soot into the compartments however carefully the windows were closed. Ladies and gentlemen in the first and second class never took off their gloves, the ladies kept their hats and veils and the gentlemen exchanged their top or bowler hats for special 'travelling caps'. On the windows there were notices: 'Leaning out of the window is prohibited.' That was not simply a stern warning. But many things in Austria were prohibited which might have been left to the common sense of the people. It seemed that the authorities had little confidence in such common sense which usually succeeded in correcting the authorities' errors of judgement. Austrians explained the difference between the extremes of others and the golden mean which was theirs. 'In America,' they said, 'everything is allowed which is not prohibited. In Russia everything is prohibited which is not expressly allowed. But in Austria everything is allowed which is prohibited.' It was the practical aspect of a negligent tyranny. And people did lean out of the windows—and the law looked the other way.

Sleeping-cars were then a new refinement of Austrian railway travel and as late as 1908 the 'Schlaf-Coupé' could be the subject of an aria, in waltz rhythm of course, in the enormously popular operetta *The Divorced Wife*. But even dining-cars were rare. For an appropriate tip the conductor arranged that at a station at lunch-time waiters were in attendance with large trays on which a whole hot three-course meal was neatly arranged. This was placed on one's knees and the balancing act which followed required a degree of dexterity of which only very experienced travellers were capable.

The journey from Prague to Vienna and back was the longest we made until July, 1914, when the family went to Trieste and took the night boat to Venice at the start of a tour of the show-places of Upper Italy as a reward for my passing the entrance examination to university. Arriving in the morning, with the enchanted city still drowsing in the haze, remains an unforgettable moment, no less unforgettable than the shock and disappointment, despair and rage when, a few hours later, shouting newspaper vendors ran through the narrow streets and crowds gathered under the arcades of St Mark's Square. War had been declared! It seemed absurd and unbelievable. Even such careful people as my father had been convinced that the crisis would resolve itself as had many crises before. While the Campanile, then quite new after its collapse, looked down on the panic below, we scrambled to the station and on to a train for home and to an uncomfortable farewell from the imperial-royal railways which were never to be the same again. But after that fateful July 28, 1914, nothing was to be the same; neither Austria nor, more particularly, Vienna.

7

The Viennese

Arriving in Vienna from Prague after seven or eight hours tired, bedraggled and dirty we were in no mood to enjoy the moment when the train thundered over the iron bridge across the Danube and came to a shrieking halt at the Franz Joseph Railway Station. But the next morning we realized that we were in a world very different from the comparative quiet of provincial Prague. Life in Vienna had another tempo, another sound, another look. The sun shone brighter, the air was clearer. There was something Italian in the air, something Southern. A street name like 'Bellaria' evoked exotic pictures and fantasies. But, strangely enough, one did not feel 'abroad'. However new and unaccustomed, it was all somehow familiar; Austrian in Viennese guise. In the few square miles of their Viennese residence the Habsburgs had achieved what they had failed to achieve in their empire. In Vienna a peculiar 'Austrian nation' had created itself, a cluster of all the nations of the Monarchy from high nobility down to roadsweeper, welded together by no more than a dialect.

Grandfather used to take me for walks in the 'Inner Town', pointing out the noble palaces then still inhabited by their noble owners and not yet turned into schools, ministries and tax collectors' offices. There were the German-Austrian Liechtenstein, Schwarzenberg, Auersperg, the Italian-Austrian Montenuovo, Collalto, Pallavicini, the Austrian-Hungarian Esterházy, Batthyány, Palffy, the Czech-Austrian Lobkowitz, Kaunitz, Kinsky, the Polish-Austrian Lanckoronski, Lubomirski, Czartoryski, even Spaniards from the olden days, Silva-Tarouca and Hoyos, or Flemings such as Clam-Gallas and Clary.

The names on the shops told the same story of the Monarchy.

There were innumerable Prohaskas and Novaks from Bohemia or Moravia, Farkas and Faludi from Hungary, Gaginelli and Grignani from Southern Tyrol, Trieste or Pola, Grzemski and Grzybicki from Cracow or Tarnow, Hribar and Matačič from Agram (later Zagreb) or Laibach (later Ljubljana) and—not necessarily in the majority—the Grubers, Lechners, Wimmers, true natives of Vienna. Tailors were Czechs, cobblers Poles, waiters Hungarians, bricklayers Italians, each nation in accordance with its natural gifts and talents. There was a large reservoir of talent on which the imperial residence could draw. The two most popular comedians of the time were Karl Blasel, true Viennese, and Alexander Girardi, born Italian, from Cortina d'Ampezzo. Among the stars of the Imperial-Royal Court Opera were the tenor Leo Slezák and the dramatic soprano Maria Jeritza, both from Moravia, and the director Gustav Mahler, a Bohemian Jew, The 'Johns' in Vienna were called 'Schani' from the Italian Giovanni, the 'Josephs' and 'Josephines' were 'Pepi' from the Italian Giuseppe and Giuseppina, even the 'Marys' were called 'Mizzi' which sounded Italian although it had no Italian origin. And, seeping through from an Italianate court into the language of the man in the street, quite a few words of Viennese dialect carried with them a hint of the sunny land to the South. A row was a 'Breugel', unconnected with the Dutch painters, but derived from the Italian 'imbroglio'; fatigue was 'Strapaz', from the Italian 'strappazzare'; to saunter was 'spazieren' from the Italian 'spaziare'.

And they all, Czechs, Poles, Hungarians, Italians spoke Viennese, the dialect which falls so softly on the ear. Philologists lump it together with Bavarian speech, but Viennese has none of the sharp edges which in Bavaria betray the proximity of the Northern varieties of the German language. There is something childish, innocent and homely about the Viennese dialect which indulges in innumerable diminutives ending with 'erl', such as 'Glaserl', a little glass, 'Sträusserl', a little bunch of flowers, even 'Lackerl', a little pool or a drop of coffee or wine derived from the Italian 'lago', a lake. These diminutives expressed not so much the size, but the affection for the object. Germans from the Reich could not even pronounce, let alone appreciate these little syllables which appeared infantile and contemptible to them. Moreover, coming from Prague one was surprised to hear the Viennese speaking not of 'Wien' but of 'Wean', which sounds like 'Vern'; and I remember that at first I could not identify the imperial city but believed they were talking of some particular district.

The Viennese were proud of a number of things, some obvious and others less so. St Stephen's—the 'Steffl'—their tongue, their city were of the first variety, the proverbial 'golden Viennese heart' of the other. Perhaps only in Bali could one make friends as easily as in Vienna—and as easily lose them. The Viennese could be almost embarrassingly friendly and unspeakably rude. In Vienna you could see more smiling faces than anywhere else but, for little reason, they could erupt into flaming fury. Viennese fickleness was almost a historic fact. Count de la Garde, ambassador, adventurer, and reporter rather than historian of the Viennese Congress, noted with amazement how the Viennese lined the streets, weeping disconsolately, when their good Emperor Franz fled before the approaching French; and how these same Viennese two days later rapturously welcomed Napoleon riding with his marshals and banners through the same streets, a spectacle which, in another costume, repeated itself 129 years later. But all this was part of the intangible 'golden Viennese heart' and if one wanted to test it one only had to ask any man for the way to any street or public building and turn in the opposite direction: whatever other business he may have had he would follow you, explain to you, call others as witnesses, and if all this did not help, he would call you all the names in the dictionary; and you would have had all the stages and transformations of the 'golden heart'.

Being generally of a childish disposition the Viennese delighted in titles. If nothing else, it made it easier for them to address people. The simple 'Herr', 'Frau' or 'Fräulein' would have satisfied neither the addressee nor the addressor and Christian names so easily and often meaninglessly used in Britain or America would have been an unacceptable familiarity. All this was easy with the nobility, but still in my time older people lamented the far-off days when every 'fiaker' or hansom cab driver would have addressed his client as 'Herr Baron' or 'Frau Baronin' or, if he happened to know his name, as 'Herr

von Roth', which was as valid an ennoblement as if the emperor
himself had conferred it. The authorities happily played the
game of titles and scattered them generously and in great
variety. University professors and Judges of the Court of Appeal
became 'Hofrat' or 'Court Councillor' and titles could accumu-
late thus: 'Hofrat Professor Doctor So-and-So', more obtrusive
than the collection of sometimes unidentifiable letters after the
names of distinguished Englishmen. High Court judges were
officially 'Oberlandesgerichtsrat' and more junior judges of the
lower courts simply 'Landesgerichtsrat', 'Rat' always meaning
'councillor'. Lower ranks such as directors of grammar schools
were 'Regierungsrat' or 'government councillor'. Prominent
businessmen were made 'kaiserlicher Rat', 'imperial councillor',
or 'Kommerzialrat', 'commercial councillor'. Meritorious
medical practitioners were 'Medizinalrat'. Of course, neither
the emperor nor the court nor the government ever made any
use of their many councillors which, considering the unhappy
ending of it all, may have been a mistake. If one were well
enough dressed and happened to wear spectacles every waiter
in a restaurant or café would address one as 'Herr Doktor'
which to credulous foreigners gave the impression that Vienna
was swarming with 'doctors'. But this predilection for titles and
the consequent stratification of society reached well down into
the lower layers of the community and was most apparent in
cafés and restaurants. One would have made a serious blunder
if one had called a waiter just 'Waiter!' as one does in other
parts of the world. For waiters, too, had their hierarchy and
their titles. In every restaurant or café there was a senior waiter
called 'Herr Ober', 'Mr Upper'. He was the man who helped
you to find the right table and the right items from the menu
and when you had finished your meal and were ready to leave
he calculated your bill without the help of paper and pencil,
took your money and gave you what change was required, all
with the dexterity of a conjurer which left you no time to check
the accuracy of the proceedings. But he did not do the actual
serving which was done by a junior. The junior, however, was
by no means called an 'Under'. He, too, was an 'Ober' but when
calling him you carefully and wisely omitted the 'Herr'. He was
just an 'Ober'. And he also had a junior, an apprentice who
served the drinks and broke the crockery and whose official title

was 'piccolo', 'the little one'. If in this way you paid proper respect to the hierarchy, they would pay proper respect to you by conferring some speculative title upon you.

And last but not least, there was the very epitome of all the qualities which made a true Viennese, the friendliness and rudeness, the good humour and the bad language—and the golden heart: the Viennese 'fiaker', the proud owner of a hansom cab and two well-groomed horses. If he had his rank on the Graben, the hub of the 'Inner Town', he was a man 'à la mode', sporting a brown check suit, a button hole and a brown bowler hat, a round face reddened by wine and wind, an inexhaustible smile, and smoking the typical 'Virginia', the most popular invention of the state tobacco monopoly, a thin ten-inch long cigar with a straw inside which was indispensable for lighting it. It was an almost ritual procedure to take out that straw and light it in order thereby to light the cigar which did not burn easily, but once burning kept the smoker company for many hours. The 'fiaker' was your friend and guide as long as you trusted him blindly. But Heaven help you if you knew something he did not know! I remember an almost public scandal when father asked the 'fiaker' who was taking us round the famous suburb of Heiligenstadt to show us the Beethoven House. 'Don't you know', the man cried, 'that there are a million people in Vienna? And you expect me that for your few shillings I should know everyone?' He was mortally offended, abruptly declared the sight-seeing tour completed, asked for his money and we had to get out. But we did then find the house ourselves although not as easily as we had expected, mainly because the local people did not quite understand the name as we pronounced it. They said, and probably are still saying, 'Bethófen', with the stress on the 'o'. And we walked the path along a winding brook which then must have looked as it did when the 'Eroica' was written nearby in the Greiner House.

8

Cafés and Cuisine

Viennese 'Gemütlichkeit' had its own institutions and establishments: the Viennese café, the Viennese 'Konditorei', and the Viennese restaurant.

The Viennese café was, so to speak, a legacy of the Turks. The Grand Vizier Kara Mustapha left it behind with all his gold and silverware and Persian rugs when, in 1683, he had to leave in an unforeseen hurry. The Viennese were soon to realise that it was the most precious of all their trophies. A Viennese called Kolschitzky—the name indicates that he was of Czech or Polish extraction—who as a spy, informer and go-between had rendered services impartially to both sides, learned from the Turks the true art of brewing coffee and when peace returned he was given a licence to open 'the first Turkish coffee house in the Christian world'. That was in 1685. The Viennese liked his coffee and Kolschitzky died a wealthy man. At the time of the great Congress there were eighty coffee houses in Vienna and in my early days there must have been eight hundred. More refined people called them 'café' but popularly they were still known as 'Kaffee Haus'.

The café was the very soul and centre of the social, artistic and commercial life of the capital. There were the elegant cafés on the Ringstrasse and the less elegant coffee houses in side streets and suburbs. In cafés or coffee houses one could have snacks such as 'Wiener Würstl', the special sausages which live and die in pairs, or scrambled eggs, or 'eggs in a glass', soft-boiled eggs tipped into a glass, or open sandwiches, beer or liqueurs. But coffee was the main purpose, the very *raison d'être* of both the 'café' and the 'Kaffee Haus'. Coffee was not only expertly brewed according to Kara Mustapha's recipe, but it required an expert to order the right type among the many varieties. The Viennese were not such primitive coffee drinkers that they did not know better than simply black or white. To start with you could ask for a cup or a glass of coffee and real connoisseurs will say that it makes a difference to the taste. Whipped cream was served with coffee as a matter of course unless you expressly excluded it or unless you ordered 'coffee with skin', meaning the thick skin of unskimmed and unpasteurized milk (and no milk was pasteurized in those days). You did not, however, simply order 'coffee with skin', but you had to be very specific: 'more white with skin', or 'dark with skin', or 'black with skin'. White coffee, too, had many shades and many names: 'cup of gold' meant a mixture of a golden colour, 'cup of brown' was similar to the Italian 'cappucino', and if you wanted black coffee with whipped cream only you ordered an 'Einspänner', which was really a figure of speech for it meant a 'fiaker' with only one horse.

Cafés were open from early morning until late at night. There were no licensing hours, but there was a closing time for all places of public entertainment marked not only by their closing, but by the last tram which had a blue light and was known as the 'Last Blue'; and if you missed it you had to walk home. Every Viennese had his favourite and permanent café where he knew the 'cafetier', the 'Obers', the 'piccolos' and the other habitués. Artists, writers, composers, librettists, singers and actors had their cafés no less than journalists, stockbrokers, businessmen and 'fiakers'. Famous works were conceived or written in the cafés and the still-famous poet Peter Altenberg, though long dead, had no other postal address than his café. There were indeed many people who spent most of their lives in the café which was comfortable, entertaining and inexpensive. For once you had ordered your coffee, served invariably with a glass of the famous ice-cold water carried by an aqueduct from the high Alps sixty miles away to the taps in Vienna, you were never molested by questions. Instead, the 'Ober'—though seldom the 'Herr Ober'—would patiently replace your glass of water whenever he thought it had become too stale to be of further use. There were masses of papers to read, daily papers, illustrated papers, the then still popular comic papers similar to but less sophisticated than London's *Punch*. And if you had exhausted all the news in the papers, the 'Ober' would usually have a few items which had not yet appeared in print. In this way you could, for a few pennies, spend a day in disproportionate comfort and keep abreast of politics, business and society. Business luncheons were almost unknown. Business partners met in the café. Even private dinner parties were rare. One met in the café where everybody would come and go as he pleased. On our visits to Vienna we always spent some considerable time at the Café Heinrichshof on the Ringstrasse opposite the opera house and while our parents chatted with their friends we children browsed through the illustrated papers with their woodcuts and drawings of great fires, earthquakes, railway disasters and shipwrecks. The world seemed full of the most interesting misfortunes and by comparison Austria, Prague and even Vienna seemed all too safe and all too dull.

In spite of their many cafés the Viennese were no coffee addicts like the Italians. One did not go to a café in order to run up a large bill. But things were very different at the 'Konditorei'. To translate 'Konditorei' by 'Tea-room' would be both misleading and inadequate. Like all Central Europeans, the Viennese drank tea only when ill in bed with a cold or after too heavy a session in a 'Konditorei'. 'Konditorei' was in fact a pastry shop with a café attached and one did not go there in order just to drink a cup of coffee and many glasses of water. The pastries were the attraction and a cup of coffee or hot chocolate with a mountain of whipped cream a mere adjunct. Indeed, the pillars on which the 'Konditorei' was built were sugar, chocolate and whipped cream, and if Viennese coffee traced its ancestry back to the Turks beleaguering Vienna, chocolate and sugar were gifts— albeit virtually the *only* gifts—of the Western Habsburg empire to the then rather neglected city on the Eastern fringe. The fashion of and the taste for 'candies' came from the luxurious court of Burgundy and from Habsburg Flanders. In 1560 Emperor Ferdinand I had a 'Court Sugar Baker' who founded a new profession and guild which spread and flourished. But chocolate was the legacy of Habsburg Mexico and came to Vienna by way of Spain. It is said that originally when the Conquistadores found the natives drinking it, it was a rather unpalatable drug. But the sugar bakers turned it into civilized man's treasured companion from the cradle to the grave. While more serious-minded potentates and governments such as the

Prussians put an embargo on this new and effeminating luxury for fear that it might sap the vigour of the nation, an Italian-Austrian court poet wrote a 'Cantata alla Cioccolata' in praise of it. With sugar, chocolate and whipped cream there was nothing to stop the culinary genius of the Viennese. By 1800 sugar bakery had reached its highest level of perfection and no wars, inflation or bankruptcy could hold it back. A certain August Dehne is the author of the most famous recipes for Viennese cakes. A street is named after him and his memory blessed and perpetuated in the 'Konditorei Demel', for in 1857 Christopher Demel took over and continued Dehne's business which with Caflisch in Naples, Hanselmann in St Moritz and Sprüngli in Zürich was among the most famous in the world. But it was by no means unique in Vienna. About 1840 one Franz Sacher baked the first 'Sacher Torte' which soon became and still is as fundamental a part of Viennese mythology as St Stephen's and the Ringstrasse. Demel's 'Konditorei' and Sacher's hotel were the places where archdukes and arch-duchesses drank their chocolate and ate 'Sacher Torte' and 'Creme Schnitten' and innumerable other products of the great artists of sugar bakery. Before the Great War those two were not the only ones. There was Lehmann, renowned 'fondants'; Scheidl for his 'petits fours'; Pirringer for his 'dragées'; and Pischinger for his own 'Pischinger Torte'. If the Viennese were a mixture of all the Austrian races, sugar bakery was as native as the River Wien which had given the city its name.

Naturally, the 'Konditorei' was not the place in which to spend a few hours. You certainly needed a little rest after your opulent 'Jause' which is the Viennese word for afternoon tea consisting of chocolate and pastries, but then you had to make room for others. And it would have been most disrespectful if you had read a paper instead of devoting all your attention to the works of culinary art set in front of you.

The other arena of culinary art was the Viennese restaurant. People sometimes try to reduce the peculiar characteristics of a town to certain fundamentals. They will say that the atmosphere of London is dominated by crowded streets, double-decker buses and the smell of roast lamb or boiled mutton; that Paris is distinguished by its boulevards, indecent posters of the

Casino de Paris and the all-pervading scent of 'Gauloises' cigarettes; and sophisticated visitors to Rome would pick out the three stones of which the Eternal City is built, the light yellow travertine, the dull, dark 'tuffo', and white marble. It is all very neat and schematic. But you could say—at least in the old days and before the 'internationlization' of cooking—that the smell of gulash belonged to the atmosphere of Vienna. Yet gulash was an imported item and an acquired taste. It really did not come from 'abroad' but only from 'Trans-Leithania', that is to say from Hungary. A few more items were imported from other 'crown lands'; 'Tiroler Knödl', Tyrolese dumplings, 'Böhmische Dalken', flat yeast cakes from Bohemia. However, sophisticated foreign dishes were unknown. Nobody, rich or poor, would eat 'escargots à la bourguignonne'. Viennese cooking was not so much sophisticated as careful and circumspect. Every soup, every meat, every gravy and particularly every sweet had to be painstakingly prepared, many pots and pans used and washing-up afterwards took as much time as the preparation itself. If English roast beef was world-famous (Yorkshire pudding was not), then it was due to the inimitable quality of the meat. Hence 'English' roast beef abroad could stand no comparison with roast beef in England. But in Vienna it was the art of cooking rather than the quality of the material which counted. Refrigerated transport had not yet been invented. Viennese housewives and chefs had to do with what the agricultural neighbourhood produced. Nonetheless a few items of Viennese cuisine had found their way into international menus, first and foremost 'Wiener Schnitzl' and 'Apfelstrudel'. But fried chicken, 'Backhendl', more recently known as 'Chicken Maryland' and spoiled by the uncalled-for addition of pineapple slices, is a native of Vienna, and 'Apfelstrudel' is but one of many varieties such as cherry strudel, poppy-seed strudel, and white cheese strudel. However, the real Viennese connoisseur did not go so much for specialities. It was the care, the taste for ordinary dishes which marked the real gourmet. 'Tafelspitz', a special cut of boiled beef with chive sauce, was the touchstone of good cooking. One went to Sachers or to Meissl and Schadn specially for this, just as one went to Schöner's Restaurant if one wanted to eat roast goose, or to 'Zur Linde' for fried chicken.

At home in Prague we did not often have the exciting

experience of being taken to a restaurant, but on our visits to Vienna it was the rule and for a few days we enjoyed the privilege of not having to eat what mother had chosen, but could choose for ourselves from a long menu. I believe one can study the character of a nation from its behaviour in a restaurant. A lonely Englishman may cursorily glance at the menu, order what first catches his eye, take out a paper or a book without allowing himself to be distracted least of all by the food on the plate in front of him, eat a few mouthfuls, drop knife and fork and so continue intermittently without prejudice to literature or food. We had been brought up very differently. There was a certain sacrificial ceremony about meals. We had to eat at a reasonable pace without pausing so that the food should not get cold; for that would have been bad for the health. To read while eating, we were told, was ill-mannered. There was no opportunity for real conversation. This had to wait for the intervals between courses or until after the meal. And above all, nothing was to be left on the plate and every piece of bread had to be eaten up. I believe that this code of conduct was the result of fastidiousness and designed to keep fastidiousness alive and sensitive. It certainly achieved it.

And so a lonely Viennese in a restaurant is the exact opposite of the lonely Englishman. He will first very carefully select his table, try here and there, like a general choosing a battlefield. He will then study the menu slowly, deliberately, circumstantially. He will, like Hercules at the crossroads, become increasingly worried as he narrows his field of choice. He will confer with the 'Ober' and call in the 'Herr Ober'. He will cross-examine them about how a dish is prepared, what ingredients and condiments are used and what vegetables may go with it. 'Two veg.', pure and simple, would never do. The 'Garnitur', as it was called, represent companions of honour which in appearance, taste and consistency will balance the main dish. The emperor himself, his master of ceremonies and his chefs could not be more concerned when preparing a banquet for a visiting monarch. Having finally chosen his meal the lonely Viennese will wait full of tension and expectation and his eyes will glow with pleasure if he is satisfied, or there will be a thundering row if he is disappointed. And this applies not only to soup and meat but also to the sweet. In other countries, and particularly in France, the high school of gourmets, the sweet is a mere coda. But in Vienna it was and is a whole finale, the closing movement of a symphony, the crowning of a good meal; one of the 'strudel' varieties or 'Palatschinken', a kind of pancake, or 'Kaiserschmarrn' which cannot be described but must be seen and tasted, and dozens of other hot sweets which you could not get in any 'Konditorei' and would not eat except for lunch or dinner.

The Viennese in particular and Austrians in general were not very fond of cheese in which France and Italy excelled. In Mondsee in the Alps near Salzburg a pleasant, mild cheese was made which you could buy in shops and order in restaurants. More famous were little rounds made from 'white cheese' in Moravian Olmütz, but they were unsuitable for consumption in public places.

And drink? Wine grew all around Vienna on the gentle slopes of the Vienna Woods, not an internationally known and competitive brand but the Viennese loved it. They would warn you not to drop it on your shoes lest it burn a hole in the leather. There were no great celebrations at vintage time in Vienna like the French 'vendanges' or the Italian 'vendemmias', but when the young wine was ready the growers in the villages on the outskirts of the city put a pole outside their cottages with a wreath of twigs and leaves as an invitation to passers-by to come in and taste their wine. That was the 'Heuriger' which has since become a great tourist attraction but was then something instituted by the Viennese for the Viennese. These once very rural and idyllic villages, Dornbach, Grinzing, Sievering, Pötzleinsdorf are now important stations on sight-seeing tours and nightly excursions, but before the Great War the Viennese gathered there in the wine-growers' back gardens on wooden benches at wooden tables, the count and the 'fiaker', the 'Kommerzialrat' and the greengrocer, bringing their own food or buying bread and salami from a man with a tray called 'Salami-Salamucci'; and they would drink the young wine and listen to the 'Schrammeln', two violins, a harmonica, a bass and a singer, the invention of one Johann Schrammel of undying memory, and to the ageless songs: 'My mother was a Viennese', 'There is only one imperial city, one Vienna', 'Vienna remains Vienna', 'There will be wine and we will no longer be'. And they would weep for happiness.

9

The Prater

The 'Heuriger' was not, of course, for us children but the 'Prater' was, that belt of grove and coppice which protected Vienna from the Danube floods. Once upon a time the 'Prater' was an imperial hunting ground and enclosed, but in 1766 it was opened to the public, and foreign visitors at the time called it 'the most remarkable sight of Vienna'. 'Prater' is a Viennese corruption of the Latin 'pratum', a field. It is a vast pleasure ground divided into three parts like Caesar's Gaul, the 'Wurstel-Prater', a permanent fair-ground, the 'Nobel-Prater', and the 'Auen', where nature itself takes over, an area of gigantic trees, lakes, rivers and swamps. Coming from town one arrived first at the 'Prater-Stern', something like the Place de l'Etoile in Paris where streets and roads converge on a victory monument—not, however, a huge triumphal arch as in Paris, but a more modest column in memory of Admiral Tegetthoff who, in 1866, hastily, unnecessarily but no less gloriously sank the Italian fleet. From there one dived straight into the hubbub of the 'Wurstel-Prater' dominated by the 'Riesenrad' or giant wheel, 190 feet in diameter with cabins turning slowly and so unfolding a wide view of the town, the Danube, the Vienna Woods and the often snow-capped peaks of the easternmost Alps in the background. It was no Viennese invention, but had been built by an Englishman in 1897. All around were a maze of booths where you could shoot with a rifle at a target and win a honeycake heart if you hit it, or you could hit a puppet with a device which measured the force of your punch. There was a 'panopticum' where you could see the murder of Czar Alexander III in wax, the Viennese variety of Punch and Judy shows, and roundabouts one of which was particularly famous because of the enormous figure of a Chinaman in the centre known to every child in Vienna as

56

'Calafatti'. Then on to the 'Grottenbahn' which to the deafening sound of an enormous organ with moving figures took you through dark grottoes where you could see the 'Wolf's Den' from Weber's opera *Der Freischütz*, Eskimos fighting polar bears and lions having arguments with elephants in the African bush. It was with a mixture of fear and fascination that we saw what our parents thought suitable for children, including the Circus Busch which was part of the fairground, but carefully *excluding* the 'Théâtre Variété' called 'Venedig in Wien', where the entertainment was less innocent.

Nearer the Danube was the 'Nobel-Prater' which was very different, a natural park of great beauty crossed in its whole length by the 'Haupt-Allee', three miles long and very wide, with riding paths on both sides, flanked by open-air cafés and restaurants among which were the exclusive 'Third Café' and the restaurant 'Constantine's Hill'. On Sunday mornings there was a *concours d'élégance* on the 'Haupt-Allee', private 'équipages' and 'fiakers' in all their finery, and Viennese society displayed its elegance in a setting that was more charming than London's Mall or Paris's Champs Elysées and as pleasing as Rome's Monte Pincio.

10

Music Old and New

These were the 'Phaeacians' of Europe and it was obviously not the purpose or mission of this German-Hungarian-Slav-Italian breed to be serious, dependable, hard-working and ambitious in any ordinary sense. They never embarked on any great money-making enterprises nor did they know the misery of real poverty. There were no great industrial undertakings. Vienna produced no heavy machinery, engines, turbines which were the misguided pride of others. Vienna's was an 'industry of taste', embroideries, tapestries, porcelain, 'galanterie' wares, small leather goods, fashions, all things which were as unnecessary as they were welcome. Indeed, the Viennese, pastmasters in the enjoyment of life, made a notable contribution to the gaiety of all civilised mankind. Paris had its uncontested, subversive charm. But there was nothing subversive in the charm of Vienna, which echoed round the world; for it expressed itself most naturally and most typically in music. Music was Vienna's great export. It broadcast the happy character of the Danube city all over the globe and made people dream of a paradise far away on the fringe of civilization.

Vienna was the capital of a shaky empire. But it was also the metropolis of an unshakeable empire of music. How this came about is something of a mystery. Few of the great or small 'Viennese' masters were Viennese. Gluck came from a village on the Austro-Bohemian border, Haydn from a village on the Austro-Hungarian frontier, Mozart hailed from Salzburg, Beethoven from Bonn and Brahms from Hamburg, Franz Lehár and Emmerich Kalmán were Hungarians, Gustav Mahler a Bohemian Jew, and one of the most Viennese of Viennese composers, Franz von Suppé or, to give him his full and correct name, Francesco Ezechiele Ermenegildo de Suppé-

Demelli, was a nephew of Donizetti and came from Spalato in Dalmatia. Of the great, only Franz Schubert and the Johann Strauss family were true Viennese.

Moreover, the tradition of music in Vienna had no deep roots in the past. It really began with Emperor Leopold I who reigned from 1658 until 1705, fought the Turks and composed music. For music this was a crucial time, for at this period it acquired the status of a great art and ceased to be a party game. As the court was to all intents and purposes Italian and the new music came from Italy, it was only natural that the most prominent 'avant-gardists' congregated in Vienna and around a monarch who was a composer in his own right. The most famous stage designer and architect of the time, Lodovico Burnacini, built the first opera house in Vienna in 1667 and performances there were sensational, all Europe talked about them and ambassadors reported on them. Musical careers were made or confirmed in Vienna where music was not just one of many displays of royal splendour like Louis XIV's 'violons du roi', but a matter of serious thought and sincere application. Since Emperor Leopold's day music was an important item in the education of little archdukes and archduchesses. His granddaughter Maria Theresa listened to the boy prodigy Mozart, her son Joseph II commissioned *Così fan tutte*, her grandson, Archduke Rudolf, was Beethoven's pupil and friend and an accomplished concert pianist.

One must not underrate the influence of a reigning family on the artistic and social climate of a country. A court will lead the fashion, the hobbies, the tendencies of the day. If the ruler and his family are first and foremost lovers of horses they will create a society of horsemen and horsewomen, of horse-breeders and race-goers. And if the ruling family loves music, society will discover its own taste and talent for the art. And this is what happened in Vienna. A passion for music spread from the Hofburg to the palaces of the nobility and from there to the man in the street, providing opportunities for musicians both foreign and native which no other place could offer. Gluck could have settled in Paris but preferred Vienna; Mozart declined an offer from Berlin although he had little reason to love the Viennese; Beethoven, once in Vienna, never left it again; and almost fifty years later Brahms still found Vienna more inspiring than any other place.

However, there is a good deal more to the musical atmosphere of Vienna than the names of Gluck, Haydn, Mozart, Beethoven, Schubert and Brahms. The men of genius were surrounded by many men of great talent. Anybody taking the trouble to look more closely at the works of the second rank of the Viennese classics—Dittersdorf, Schenk, Hummel, Stadler, Gyrowetz, Worzischek, Krommer, Eybler or Eberl—will be surprised at their quality. In their own time they were widely appreciated, so much so that after the first performance of his Fifth Symphony Beethoven was advised by the critic of the *Wiener Salonblatt* to take lessons from Eberl should he intend to write another symphony in C minor. And what immortal credit is due to the violinist Schuppanzigh who with his colleagues first played Beethoven's last string quartets? One has to view the whole scene in order to appreciate the standing and charm of Vienna in this most decisive epoch of the musical art which, in its own way, was comparable to that of Florence in painting, architecture and sculpture during the fifteenth century.

But the music of the great Viennese classics proved a barrier to further development. Although the fickle Viennese forgot Mozart for a time and did not appreciate Schubert in his lifetime (which was not altogether the fault of the Viennese), the music which followed the great epoch did not find a home in Vienna, even though the Viennese became wildly enthusiastic about Rossini, Bellini, Donizetti, and later about Meyerbeer, Halévy and the earlier Wagner (between 1870 and 1900 *Tannhäuser* had 238, and *Lohengrin* 288 performances), the honour and glory of the newest 'new' music went to Paris, Munich and Berlin. In Vienna there was a tendency to keep the new 'avant-garde' at arm's length. If it had not been for Brahms Viennese music after Beethoven and Schubert would have made an insignificant impact and some would say that Brahms's popularity was due to his 'traditionalism' and to his opposition to Wagner whose later works were received with marked coolness. Vienna let the honour of first performing *Tristan und Isolde* slip by without regret; Anton Bruckner had to earn his laurels in Germany; and neither Hugo Wolf nor Gustav Mahler had many friends in Vienna. No wonder that the Viennese Arnold Schoenberg had his revolutionary *Pierrot lunaire* first performed in Berlin and when, in 1913, the Vienna Philharmonic played

Stravinsky's *Petrushka* which had already been performed in Paris, Berlin and even Budapest, he was outraged at the performance, called the Viennese barbarians who did not know Debussy, and has hated Vienna ever since. Certainly, by the beginning of this century, when Brahms was dead, Vienna was no longer in the mainstream of musical adventure, and of all the new composers only Richard Strauss had made the grade with the Viennese.

The Viennese should have been sorry that they had thus fallen from grace, but they were not. If one could not hear the latest music in Vienna, one could at least hear the best performances of the finest 'old' music, the constant and untiring care of which had produced a standard of performance unequalled anywhere in the world. In this the Viennese were as fastidious as they were with their food and their pleasures. All the hue and cry about new music which came from Paris and Berlin was met in Vienna with the cold smile of superior knowledge and expertise of the music which was bound to survive all the innovators and was to them the music of the future no less than the music of the past.

The Court Opera was the most conspicuous temple of music in Vienna. I vividly remember my first visit. We should have heard *Don Giovanni* (or *Don Juan* as it was called, for every opera was sung in German). It was the opera which I then knew best, having heard it in Prague both in German and Czech. But when we arrived in the evening, red leaflets were displayed above the box office and at every entrance saying that 'Frau Kammersängerin So-and-So' was indisposed and that Berlioz' *Benvenuto Cellini* would be given instead of *Don Juan*. I have hated Berlioz ever since. But I remember happier occasions; the *Barber of Seville* with the famous coloratura soprano Selma Kurz who sang like a bird though she did not look like one; *Rienzi* with the tenor Erik Schmedes of Bayreuth fame; Meyerbeer's *Huguenots* which was still a great favourite; Goldmark's *Queen of Sheba* with the equally famous Elisa Elizza in the leading part; Wilhelm Kienzel's *Evangelimann*, once enormously popular all over the German-speaking world and, I understand, still alive; *Meistersinger* with the tenor Leo Slezak, then very young and at his ringing best, singing his Prize Song at 11 p.m. with the same vigour as he had started five hours earlier. There was all the panache of a Court Opera. The Hof-Loge, or Court Box, was never empty and although the old emperor was no theatre-goer any more, some members of the arch-house were always there. After all, the Court Opera was no state opera but the emperor's own and what deficit there was was paid out of his private purse and not by the tax-payer. The singers on the posters and in the programmes were not simply called by their names but it was always 'Herr Betetto' or 'Frau Kiurina' or Fräulein Jeritza' and if they had a title that title was naturally mentioned too, such as 'Herr Kammersänger Erik Schmedes' or 'Frau Kammersängerin Elisa Elizza'. Needless to say, everybody from the director down to the usher was 'k.k.'—imperial-royal. The public was not as ostentatious in their dress, jewellery or behaviour as at the Scala in Milan, but one could feel the expertise of this audience and the cheaper the seats or standing enclosures in the uppermost gallery, the more expert were the listeners. The many officers in dress uniform with softly ringing spurs and sabres gave every evening the appearance of a gala performance. The ushers in brown gold-braided uniforms were as dignified as archdukes, but accepting a tip for reserving hats and coats after the performance was not beneath their dignity. (Police regulations did not allow overcoats or umbrellas to be taken into the auditorium.)

The Court Opera and its singers were as popular in Vienna as opera and singers were in Italy. Every barber or 'fiaker' could tell you the latest rows or the latest of Leo Slezak's frequent jokes. Gustav Mahler was no longer director and nobody was sorry about his departure. He had been a perfectionist with the motto 'tradition is negligence' and the Viennese did not like it. They called him Gustav 'Malheur' and stories were told how he sacked and sent into retirement everyone who did not blindly submit to his dictatorial rule which caused the pension fund to run out of money so that the emperor himself had to rescue it. The next 'k.k. Hofopern-Direktor' was Felix von Weingartner, the most handsome, most elegant and aristocratic director any opera house could have. And he was also the chief conductor of the orchestra.

For in the pit of the Court Opera sat the Vienna Philhar-monic Orchestra. It had a treble existence. In the evening at the Opera it was called 'the Imperial-Royal Court Opera

Orchestra' and as such it had a long history going back to the seventeenth century and to Emperor Leopold I. On Sunday mornings at the Hofburg-Kapelle, the chapel of the imperial palace, the same orchestra, or a section of it, played at high mass and was simply called 'Court Orchestra'; and its ancestry reached even further back into the past for more than four hundred years. And later on Sunday mornings, at 12 noon, the same orchestra gave its ordinary and its extraordinary concerts in the large hall of the 'Musikverein' and was then called 'the Vienna Philharmonic Orchestra'. And in this capacity they were a fairly recent institution. They gave their first concert on Sunday, March 28, 1842, at 12.30 p.m. at the Imperial-Royal Redoute, conducted by Otto Nicolai, then first conductor of the Opera and composer of the still popular *Merry Wives of Windsor*. Artists in those days were more generous or more robust than they are now. That first concert of the Vienna Philharmonic began with Beethoven's Seventh Symphony, followed by an aria from Cherubini's *Fanisca* and Beethoven's concert aria 'Ah, perfido'. After the interval there was Beethoven's Third Leonora Overture, Mozart's aria 'Non temer', a violin solo with orchestra 'La Romanesca', a duet from Cherubini's *Medea*, and finally Beethoven's overture *The Consecration of the House*. So the newly-formed orchestra made a great effort to ingratiate itself with its first audience. With true Viennese sensibility, the second concert, six months later, was considerably shorter. But the Vienna Philharmonic Orchestra has kept to the traditional time for its concerts and every year gives its 'Nicolai Concert' in memory of its first conductor.

A musical Sunday in Vienna was then truly unique: at 11 a.m. one went to the Hofburg-Kapelle where the Vienna Choir Boys sang and the Vienna Philharmonic played a mass by Haydn, Mozart, Schubert or Bruckner, or Beethoven's Mass in C (though not the *Missa Solemnis* which was banned from church). The Vienna Choir Boys were not yet a commercial undertaking, but the same as in Haydn's or Schubert's days, boys of poor parents with good voices who received general and musical education and sang at the services at St Stephen's which were usually purely vocal with organ accompaniment; and at the Imperial Chapel where mass was given all its musical glory, although besides Beethoven's Mass in D, some of Haydn's and

Mozart's masses such as the latter's 'Sparrow Mass' were excluded by the Church authorities as being too 'worldly'.

From the service at the Hofburg-Kapelle one went straight to the Musikverein and the Sunday concert of the Vienna Philharmonic, usually conducted by Weingartner, not so much commanding the orchestra as caressing the legacy of the 'golden age' of Viennese music. He had beautifully round gestures and an inimitable way of stretching the little finger away from the others. Coming from Prague the repertoire seemed rather conservative and slightly monotonous, but the sound of the orchestra, the sweetness of the strings and the roundness and fullness of the brass and woodwind, were a revelation. By comparison, Prague orchestras sounded sharp and edgy and the horns wobbly and uncertain. I remember a programme note of the Vienna Philharmonic which quoted Wagner as saying, after he had conducted the *Tristan* Prelude in Vienna: 'This is much nicer than I composed it.' I do not know whether Weingartner would today be considered as good a conductor as he then was, but the way he led from the Scherzo to the last movement of Beethoven's Fifth Symphony was an experience never to be repeated again. It was like the slow opening of a gate from a dark corridor into heaven itself.

Those were the early days of travelling orchestras and Weingartner was the first to take an orchestra on tour abroad. But the Vienna Philharmonic did not really need this kind of publicity. The world knew that it was a superb orchestra and its competitors in Berlin and New York were still a good way behind.

To round off the musical Sunday in Vienna one went in the evening to the Court Opera. All the theatres played on Sundays and were closed only on Christmas Eve and Good Friday. Our visits to Vienna were so planned that we were present at three musical sessions and at the end of the day we had arrived at the sweet tiredness of deep satisfaction one could not have found anywhere else in the world.

Like the opera, the Vienna Philharmonic Orchestra was one of the most popular institutions with the Viennese. It was a microcosm of the Monarchy with every nationality represented and every language spoken. There were very few young men among its ranks; most of its members were bearded, middle-aged 'professors' and all of them were great experts. They were merciless with young conductors and tested them by playing wrong notes, and if the newcomer did not notice such errors, he had no chance of ever being engaged. There were great humorists among them and their jokes made the round in Vienna. There was at the time a Carinthian composer of very simple and very popular folk-like songs, all in C major. Every housemaid sang his 'Alone am I, alone like a stone in the road'. Angered by such cheap popularity the 'Konzertmeister', or leader of the Philharmonic, Joseph Hellmesberger, famous for his beautiful tone and for his sharp tongue, said to a friend: 'Have you heard? Thomas Koschat has sold the black keys of his piano. He does not need them.' At a rehearsal with a new conductor who kept interrupting the orchestra by asking for a passage to be repeated over and over again, the solo cellist Friedrich Buxbaum rose and told him: 'If you interrupt us once more we shall play as you conduct.' Or when the solo viola Anton Ruzitska was asked what a new conductor would conduct at a forthcoming concert, he replied: 'I do not know what he will conduct, but *we* will play the Jupiter Symphony.' Or Arnold Rosé, Hellmesberger's successor as Konzertmeister, once said to a new conductor at the end of a performance of Mozart's *Entführung aus dem Serail*: 'Ah, good evening, Herr Kapellmeister, I had not noticed that you were here.' These and many other jokes contributed to the popularity of the orchestra. It was the pride and joy of all Vienna.

Waltzes and Operettas

All this was still exquisite fruit from old trees. But new trees had grown in Vienna's musical orchard with a coarser but equally delicious yield. The mantle of Viennese music had fallen on the shoulders of Johann Strauss, his contemporaries and successors and new glory spread the fame of the Danube City all over the world.

The visitor to Vienna would have looked in vain for the famous old theatres hallowed by the first performances of Mozart's operas and of Beethoven's *Fidelio*. The old Kärntnertor Theatre had been replaced by the new Court Opera and the old Burg Theatre by the new Hofburg Theatre. But he could still find 'Papageno Street', and in this street a gate with a carving above a closed entrance: Papageno with his birdcage playing his chimes. This gate was all that was left of the old 'Theater an der Wien' where *The Magic Flute* was first performed. Mozart knew the gate though he did not know the carving which was placed there ten years after his death by Emanuel Schikaneder, librettist and first Papageno, in gratitude for a best-seller. The theatre itself, rebuilt and enlarged, still existed behind the closed gate and was no less famous than its more modest and suburban predecessor. In fact, it was one of the most famous places in the world of the musical theatre, the birthplace of many of the great Viennese operettas. It had a rival in another part of the city, on the other side of the Danube canal, the one arm of the river which ventured into the town. That was the Carl Theatre, built in 1847 to replace an older theatre where generations of Viennese had been entertained rather than uplifted. And that was the other birthplace of famous operettas.

There had been, before my time, yet another more recent theatre on the newly laid-out Ringstrasse, the Ring Theatre, but nobody liked to be reminded of it for it had been the scene of one of the worst disasters in stage history. On December 7, 1881 at 7 o'clock in the evening, when the curtain rose for the second performance of Offenbach's posthumous opera *The Tales of Hoffmann*, fire broke out and 384 people were burnt or trampled to death. The Ring Theatre was never rebuilt and its place was taken, almost symbolically, by the new headquarters of police.

In my time Viennese operetta and everything that went with it had its second flowering. Older people spoke nostalgically of the bygone days of the 'classical' Viennese operetta. Johann Strauss, Suppé and Millöcker, the three classics of the 'classical' operetta and counterparts of Haydn, Mozart and Beethoven, were dead. They represented the heroic age of Viennese light music for they had to do battle with their French rivals, with Offenbach, Lecocq, Audran, Waldteufel. It was like the battle of Aspern all over again; the French were not beaten but halted. French operettas had the same subversive charm as Paris, their wit was sharp, their couplets acid, they leaned heavily on sarcasm and caricature, the French 'valse lente' was slow, languid, sensual. The Viennese on the other hand preferred a hearty laugh without any hidden meaning and an equally serious tear, their waltzes were faster, bolder, more temperamental and musically more elaborate, even complicated in their clever syncopation which never disturbed their swing and lilt. Johann Strauss's 'Blue Danube', 'Voices of Spring', 'Tales from the Vienna Woods' were little symphonic poems in waltz rhythm to be played, sung and danced and the whole world played and danced to them although only the Viennese, or some of them, knew the words which went with them. The 'Blue Danube' was originally written for men's choir and orchestra, 'Voices of Spring' for coloratura soprano! These three giants of the Viennese operetta and the Viennese waltz represented the champagne years of the imperial city, the years after the débâcle of 1866 when, freed from all the responsibilities of a great power, Austrians could really enjoy life. Strauss's *Fledermaus* was first heard in 1874, Suppé's *Boccaccio* in 1879, Millöcker's *Bettelstudent* in 1882, Strauss's *Gipsy Baron* in 1885. But these were only the highlights. In between there were one or two new operettas every year from the 'second rank' of classics, Zeller, Ziehrer, Reinhardt, which were more than local successes.

In 1899 Johann Strauss died and with him, so older people thought, there died another great epoch of Viennese music. What followed, they believed, was a period of decline and the new composers were no more than stragglers. But what stragglers! In 1902 Franz Lehár's first operetta, *Der Rastelbinder* (*The Tinker*), was first performed. For a straggler it was no mean achievement. But it was not as Viennese as the 'classical' operetta. Lehár himself was Hungarian and his music was more 'Austrian' than Viennese, his waltzes spoke Viennese with a Hungarian accent, but their speech was as fluent as that of any Viennese. Indeed, this second flowering of the Viennese operetta was truly *Austrian*, 'cosmopolitan' Austrian using all the colours of the colourful Monarchy. In 1905 *The Merry Widow* was first performed, a world success unparalleled by any of its predecessors. How the original French comedy was 'Austrianized' by Lehár's librettists may help the reader to understand the old empire. In Meilhac's comedy, *L'Attaché*, a young and fabulously rich widow, Madeleine de Palmer, meets in Paris the ambassador of a little German principality who wants to marry her to his attaché, Count Prachs, so that her fortune may remain in the principality. For the purpose of the 'Viennese' operetta the scene had still to be Paris because there was no 'Maxim' in Vienna, and if one wanted to be *really* naughty one had to go to Paris. But what then happens in this operetta version of Paris is truly *Austrian*. A dull little German principality would not do. It was accordingly transformed into the 'principality of Pontevedro', which sounds very much like Montenegro, that long-lost, long-forgotten principality in the mountains towering above the 'Bocche di Cattaro' on the Adriatic, bordering on the southernmost corner of the Monarchy. Montenegro was larger than Monaco, but one medium-sized house in Monte Carlo was probably worth more than the whole of Montenegro put together. However, not long before *The Merry Widow* was written, the 'prince' of Montenegro had made himself a king and his country a kingdom, a shepherd kingdom ruled by a shepherd king installed in a 'palace' which was not much more than a farmhouse. But with a broad, jovial smile on his round face adorned by a bushy black moustache, in his Turkish costume with blue jacket, blue baggy trousers, moccasins with upturned points and a broad red belt with a revolver and a knife always handy he was a popular figure in that part of the world—and beyond, for one of his black-haired, fiery-eyed daughters married the 're bambino', little King Victor Emanuel III of Italy, and so became a real queen. The attaché of this romantic country could not be a 'Count Prachs', but was re-named Danilo Danilovitch. There had in fact been a Prince Danilo of Montenegro before *The Merry Widow* who unfortunately, though not surprisingly, had been assassinated. Such things tended to happen in any Balkan country. Having Austrianized the background, the librettists had to do the same with the central figure. No girl in any part of Austria or Hungary would have been christened 'Madeleine' nor were there any 'Palmers' to be found. So, in Lehár's operetta she became Hanna Glawari which is not characteristically Viennese, but rather Croat and, therefore, not too remote from Danilo.

Having been thus Austrianized, the characters do not indulge in peppery couplets, chansons and can-cans but in Viennese waltzes and Hungarian 'csárdas'. *The Merry Widow* swept the board. But competitors were soon in the field; two years later came Oscar Straus's *Waltz Dream*, more genuinely Viennese, and Leo Fall's *Dollar Princess*, Viennese in an ominously American setting; another year later they were followed by the same Leo Fall's *Geschiedene Frau* and in 1909 by Lehár's *Count of Luxemburg*, all of them overflowing with melodies which bands, dance orchestras and even pianolas played around the world.

Such was Vienna's inimitable kind of atmospheric export from the 'Theater an der Wien' and from the Carl Theatre, from the Café Central in Vienna and from the Café Zauner in Bad Ischl. The words may often have been stupid and contrived, but they had all the ingredients which made life worth living; love, money, simple jokes and, at the end of the second act, a few tears with a large dose of sentimentality. And the music was as happy as only music can be. For the world at large a picture of a paradise down there on the Danube, of a romantic city of beautiful girls and smart young men, of good humour and sweet music, innocent of troubles and worries, an island of 'Phaeacians' as only Homer—and Lehár—could describe it.

Serious-minded people frowned upon this late 'renaissance' in the metropolis of music, home of Gluck, Mozart, Haydn, of Beethoven, Schubert and Brahms. In the early nineteenth century music had split in two, serious or high-brow music had separated from light and popular music and Vienna, they said, had chosen the wrong one. Nor, in their opinion, could the masters of the second flowering of Viennese or Austrian music measure up to the greater masters of the first.

Other critics, not only abroad, said that the picture of the paradise on the Danube was no more than a mirage. They spoke of ominous signs of decadence which manifested itself in the rejection of everything new in music, in architecture, in painting. The Viennese laughed at the 'Sezession', an exhibition building in the 'art nouveau' style and rejected the 'art nouveau' pictures and sculptures of Gustav Klimt. But they liked Arthur Schnitzler's 'decadent' plays at the Hofburg Theatre, they were thoughtless pleasure-seekers lazing in a sun they believed could never set while somewhere in an unknown place on the other side of the Atlantic a new 'light' music was rising, the music of want and poverty without illusion; and diplomats and generals were busy plotting their collision course on the map of old-fashioned Europe, collision with happiness which came from the very land where it was first to end.

BUDAPEST AND THE HUNGARIANS

I

Across the Leitha

We have met Hungarians, but have not yet crossed the river Leitha into 'Trans-Leithania' or Hungary, the other half of the Double Monarchy.

'Double Monarchy' does not refer to the Habsburg double eagle. That double eagle, a heraldic beast with one body and two heads looking rapaciously right and left, East and West, was a very old bird, while the Double Monarchy was a comparatively recent invention. It was, in fact, a considerable understatement, for the Habsburg empire was in fact a multiple monarchy as is shown in the title of the emperor, of his imperial and royal majesty. He was 'Emperor of Austria, King of Hungary, Bohemia, of Dalmatia, Croatia, Slavonia, Galicia, Lodomeria and Illyria', which made eight real kingdoms—or, to be precise, nine, for he was also the imaginary and inconsequential King of Jerusalem. In addition, he was Archduke of Austria, Duke of Styria, Carinthia, Carnia and Bukovina, Grandduke of Transylvania, Margrave of Moravia and of twenty-nine other countries, some of which like Tuscany and Lorraine, Habsburg and Kyburg, had long since been lost.

But all this multiplicity was overshadowed by a more modern duality, for in 1867 the Monarchy was officially split into two halves, Austrian and Hungarian. After the defeat of 1866, when the emperor and the empire were too weak to resist, the Hungarians forced this 'duality' on him by what became known as the 'Hungarian Settlement', the settlement of almost exactly 240 years of quarrel and strife.

At the time of the 'Settlement' and until the 'Collapse', Hungary was a fairly large and compact country with a population of about nineteen million people. In the North it reached as far as the Carpathian Mountains comprising what later was called 'Slovakia', but was then known as Upper Hungary. In the East it included the mountainous region of Transylvania and in the South and South-East it extended through Croatia and Slavonia to Fiume on the Adriatic. Almost two-thirds of the country were inhabited by Slavs and Rumanians with a sprinkling of Germans, although the Hungarians were disinclined to take any notice of them. Of the Slavs we shall have more to say and the Germans are of little importance. But the Rumanians who had their own kingdom beyond the borders of Transylvania were a very special and somewhat mysterious race. They still are the only people in South-East Europe who speak a 'Latin', though much corrupted, language. Their origin has never been satisfactorily explained. Their own historians believe they are the descendants of Roman legionaries left behind by Emperor Trajan after he had defeated and contained the Dacians. Others, less respectfully, say that they were gipsies of the old Roman empire who roamed the region of present-day Albania until they were pushed North and settled in the Danube areas of Valachia and Moldavia where they were subdued by the Turks and eventually liberated when the Turks were thrown back across the river.

But who are the Hungarians? They were late-comers to Europe. Germans and Slavs and perhaps Rumanians had already established themselves and the Germans in particular were already largely christianized when the Magyars arrived from an unknown East. They gave themselves the two alternative names of 'Ogurs', or Hungarians, and 'Megy-eris', or Magyars. They were an outlandish and sinister race. To this day they speak a language whose vocabulary and grammar has no affinity with either Germanic or Roman languages. To the foreigner it seems a haphazard accumulation of vowels and consonants forming very long words and the many accents seem to indicate that it had to be forced into the straitjacket of the Latin alphabet. In the 'crown lands' of Austria it was not taught and I have never learned it. It used to be said that if you could say 'Dov'è la piazza Vittorio Emanuele?' you could travel through the whole of Italy without any greater knowledge of the language. In Hungary you might have had to know more: 'Fekete', black or, 'fehér', white coffee, 'fizetni', the bill, and 'köszönöm szépe', thank you, because you did not get much further than a café.

Philologists say that there is a distant relationship with the Finns
in the North who once occupied a much larger territory than
today, and the Turks who themselves are a mixture of various
races. But Finns, Hungarians and Turks cannot understand
each other and what fraternization there was at times between
the Hungarians and the Turks was due to politics and not to
family connections. Zoltán Kodály, the composer, searching for
the uncertain origin of his people through the medium of folksong, found communities on the middle Volga, deep in Russia,
who did not speak anything like Hungarian but whose folksongs
have the same characteristics as old Hungarian folksongs; and
that is as good as any archaeological discovery.

In fact, the Hungarians or Magyars were the third batch of
intruders from the East in the first millennium A.D. The first, as
is known, were the Huns who came in A.D. 375. To the tall,
fair-haired Germans they appeared singularly ugly, small, dark-
skinned, black-haired, with slanting eyes and bent legs. They
were ferocious horsemen, merciless killers and ruthless robbers.
They were nomads who made the then empty former Roman
province of Pannonia their headquarters rather than their
home. They did not care for conquering lands, but only for
robbing them. They raided Germany, Italy and France and
their most famous chieftain or king, Attila, terrorized all
Europe until, in A.D. 451, the Huns were decisively beaten and
thereafter disappeared like ghosts, leaving nothing behind them
but the most infamous name in all history.

A little more than a hundred years later another band of
Asians, the Avares, followed in the steps of the Huns, crossing
the Carpathian mountains from the East and making empty
Pannonia their headquarters once more. They were better
organized and less cruel than the Huns but they, too, lived on
their raids rather than by working the land and building permanent dwellings. Whether their move into Europe was connected with the Huns has never been established. Their raids,
though less extended and less devastating, were enough for
Charlemagne to mount two campaigns against them and after
their final defeat in A.D. 796 they too disappeared. Archaeo-
logists have found their tombs and their ring-shaped camps in
modern Hungary.

And another hundred years later a third wave of Asians

arrived, our Hungarians, and settled in the empty, nameless plain between the rivers Danube and Tisza. 'Hungarian' is reminiscent of 'Hun'. Hungarian historians believe there to be a connection between them and they not only treasure the memory of King Attila, who must have been a formidable character, but they are at some pains to redeem his honour and the honour of his people. They were not as bad, they say, as German and French chroniclers portrayed them and the Hungarians, their cousins, were an example of 'Asian tolerance'. All the same, the Hungarians may not have been as bad as the Huns, but they were certainly worse than the Avares. They were at a disadvantage in coming so late to Europe. When the other nations and races started on their road to civilization, they were all more or less on the same level of noble savagery. But compared with their neighbours, the Hungarians were a few hundred years in arrears. Like the Huns and the Avares they were nomads, lived in tents, bred horses and went raiding. They ravaged Bavaria, burned Pavia and laid waste Southern France. Opera-goers may recall King Henry's words in Wagner's *Lohengrin*: 'O Lord, protect us from the Hungarians' wrath!' In Vienna King Henry was not allowed to say that lest the Trans-Leithanians should take exception. But it was this same King Henry I of Germany, Henry 'The Fowler', who won a series of victories over the roaming hordes of Hungarians, culminating in A.D. 955 in the massacre near Augsburg in Bavaria where, according to the chronicle of St Gall, 100,000 Hungarians were slaughtered and only seven escaped to tell the tale at home.

More docile and adaptable than their forerunners, the Hungarian chieftain and his elders learned the lesson that the happy days of raiding and robbing were over and that the nomads had to settle on the land, till the fields, work and pray. To go back whence they had come was no longer a possible alternative. The Hungarians had seen too much of Europe to return to a wilderness they could no longer remember. King Vajk, direct descendant of chief Arpád who had occupied 'Hungary', adopted Christianity and the name Stephen, enforced catholicism among his people, was made 'Apostolic King' by the Pope, was canonized and became the patron saint of his country. So, in the year A.D. 1000, this Asiatic people entered the family of European nations. By that time most of the Magyars must have been already near-European in appearance for they used to bring back from their raids not only gold and valuables, but also women. King Stephen himself married a Bavarian princess and established himself in the capital Buda on the Danube—a fortress, a palace and a church which dominated the fertile and prosperous countryside.

The royal house of the Arpáds was far less lucky than the Habsburgs. Hungary did not inherit; it was inherited. In the year 1300, after the last of the Arpáds, the French Anjous arrived, then the Bohemian Luxemburgs, then the Polish Jagiellos. The Hungarians did not seem to mind or, more probably, their magnates were quite happy with their foreign rulers. But there followed, in 1458, a short interlude with an indigenous king, Matthias, who called himself Corvinus, the 'Raven King'. He was the son of a national hero at a time when the Hungarians really needed one. Constantinople had fallen to the Turks, who then pressed northward towards Hungary. King Matthias's father, John Hunyádi, distinguished himself in many battles with the first Turks on Hungarian soil. As children we knew John Hunyádi or, as the Hungarians say, Hunyádi János very well. His picture appeared on the label of a very popular laxative named after him, a peculiar way of commemorating so valiant a warrior. But that natural laxative came from a source in Transylvania and Hunyádi János was 'Prince of Transylvania' which may perhaps justify the apparent absurdity. In passing, I should explain that Hungarians always put the family name first and the Christian name afterwards. They would not say Franz Liszt, Béla Bartók or John Háry, but Liszt Ferenc, Bartók Béla and Háry János. Thus the hero of Kodály Zoltán's celebrated opera is not 'János' but 'Háry'.

King Matthias Corvinus did very well for his country and his people. He founded universities, knew about the new movement of the Renaissance, and waged successful wars. For a time he even occupied Vienna and might have satisfied the gravitational force of the Danube Basin had he lived longer and had a son like him. But he was denied both and when he died the Polish Jagiellos succeeded once more to the throne of St Stephen. Then the Turks came in earnest. On August 29, 1526, the Hungarians were crushed at Mohács in Southern Hungary and their king killed, leaving the Habsburgs the only legitimate successors to the Hungarian (and Bohemian) crown. It was the birthday of the Danube Monarchy; and it was an unhappy day. The Hungarians regard it as the blackest day in their whole history. Even now a Hungarian who loses his sweetheart or his money will comfort himself by saying: 'We have lost more at Mohács.'

The Hungarians hated the Habsburgs. They thought that they had been caught between two evils and often enough when they had to choose between the most Christian emperor and the most Mohammedan sultan they chose the sultan. Three years after Mohács the Turks stood at the gates of Vienna and were beaten back. But they stormed the fortress of Buda which for the next 150 years was to be the seat of a Turkish Pasha ruling two-thirds of Hungary as a Turkish province or 'pashalik', while the remaining third groaned under the Habsburg yoke.

To liberate Hungary from the heathens was the Habsburgs' holy duty. But their efforts found the Hungarians, or more precisely the Hungarian magnates, in a dilemma. They, too, wished to be liberated, but least of all by the Habsburgs. In 1664 the Austrians defeated the Turks, but a Hungarian rebellion prevented them from exploiting their victory. And in 1683 it was a Hungarian rebel leader who started a new war with Austria and showed the Turks the way to Vienna once more. However, this time the inevitable happened: the Turks were beaten at the gates of Vienna, Austrians stormed Turkish Buda and raised the Habsburg flag. Within thirteen years Hungary was liberated and no Turk was left on Hungarian soil. It was an event to be celebrated. But the Hungarians did not celebrate, nor were they grateful. One Franz Rákocsi, another prince of Transylvania, issued a manifesto, declared the Hungarian throne vacant and began a war against Austria and the Habsburgs which ended only eight years later with Rákocsi's escape to France. Apart from illustrating the mood of the liberated Hungarians, this episode would hardly be worth mentioning, had not the name Rákocsi subsequently become known all over the world. Many listeners to Berlioz' version of the 'Rákocsi March' may have wondered how this rousing and defiant piece got its name. It was in fact, this same Rákocsi's own march and dates from the beginning of the eighteenth century. And only Hungarians can march to its complicated and syncopated rhythm.

The relationship between Austria and Hungary remained uneasily poised until 1848, the year of revolutions. In Hungary, however, it took the form not simply of revolution, but of full-scale war. Once more the emperor was deposed and a Hungarian national army, the 'Honvéd', took the field. The poet Alexander Petöfi provided patriotic poems, and the politician Ludwig Kossuth a political programme, based on complete independence from Austria. It took the intervention of an imperial Russian corps to put the rising down. Petöfi died in action and Kossuth fled the country for ever. Thirteen of the rebel leaders were executed and Austrian rule was restored. Small wonder that both the magnates and the ordinary people brooded angrily on these events, on the emperor in Vienna, and on his chief executioner Prince Windischgrätz.

But then came the crucial year 1866. When the Prussian army invaded Bohemia, Empress Elizabeth, Franz Joseph's wife, fled to Budapest and even the most rabid anti-Habsburgs were charmed by her beauty (Hungarians never could resist the charms of a beautiful woman). More than a hundred years before they had been overwhelmed by the charm of Empress Maria Theresa when she came with tears in her eyes and her baby son in her arms, begging for their help against these same Prussians. Although they stubbornly insisted on calling her their 'king' because St Stephen, 750 years before, had decreed that no woman should sit on the Hungarian throne, they cried 'Éljen!', 'Vivat!', and gave her the troops and the money she needed. And now, faced with another beautiful empress and a defeated emperor, they agreed to settle their 340-year-old quarrels once and for all. This was the 'Settlement', the solemn document which split the multiple into a 'double' monarchy, an unusual but characteristically Austro-Hungarian mixture of fact and make-belief.

Hungary was recognized as a kingdom in its own right with the emperor of Austria as king, not by right but by automatic renewal, on condition that he came to Budapest in person to be crowned with St Stephen's crown in St Matthew's Church and to ride up the grassy hill in front of the church and in full view of the city, and there brandish St Stephen's sword in the four directions of the compass as a sign that he would defend the country against all comers—including himself. His coronation duly took place in 1867 and the most convincing sign of complete reconciliation was that Count Julius Andrássy himself put the crown on the emperor's head, the same man who, twenty years before, had been sentenced to death in his absence and had his name nailed to the gallows. In the years to follow he was to become one of the emperor's most influential advisers.

Hungary was given complete home rule. It was to have its own cabinet of ministers and its own parliament, the 'commons' and the 'magnates'. The state language and the language of parliament which until then had been Latin was to be Hungarian with no consideration given to Slovaks, Ruthenians, Rumanians, Germans, Croats or Slovenes. The coat of arms was St Stephen's crown and cross; the state colours were red, white and green; the 'Honvéd', the home army which had fought the Austrians in 1848 and had been disbanded after the defeat, was re-formed; and the 'Rákocsi March' was adopted as its signature tune without causing any embarrassment on either side.

But the ministries of foreign affairs and war remained common to both halves of the Monarchy, and as the ministry of war required a substantial share of the tax-payer's money there had to be a common ministry of finance as well.

This caused some complications. Those privileges which had been granted to the Hungarian half had to be matched by parallel institutions on the Austrian side. So Austria, too, had to be given its own cabinet of ministers, its own parliament, the 'deputies' and the 'Herren', and its own home army or 'Landwehr'. There was no need, however, for a new coat of arms, colours or language. All these remained as they had been for so many centuries.

But the 'duality' of institutions created some niceties which the visitor from abroad either did not notice or could not understand. All institutions which were purely *Hungarian* were 'Royal Hungarian', abbreviated 'k.u.', 'königlich ungarisch'. That was easy and obvious. The 'k.u. Ministry of Education' was unmistakably the Hungarian ministry. The corresponding *Austrian* institutions were 'Imperial-Royal', abbreviated 'k.k.', 'kaiserlich-königlich'; for example, the 'k.k. Ministry of Education'. And this was not so obvious. But—and this was the ultimate finesse—common institutions were 'Imperial *and* Royal', 'k.u.k.', 'kaiserlich *und* königlich', such as the 'k.u.k. Army', where the inconspicuous word 'and' made all the difference. It was all very delicately contrived and gave the Austrians the feeling that they had lost nothing in the deal and convinced the Hungarians that St Stephen himself could not have done better. After all the years of bitterness Austrians and Hungarians fell into each other's arms and professed to be happy and satisfied. Only Kossuth remained irreconcilable and remained in exile until his death.

It was not easy to understand why such a 'Settlement' should have taken so long. The Hungarians had always been popular in Vienna and the Viennese had never particularly been unpopular in Budapest. What ill-feelings there had been were strictly confined to politicians on both sides and never affected the ordinary man in the street. Hungarians were entertaining, voluble, colourful, just the type the Viennese preferred to the dull and stodgy Germans from the Reich. The accent with which Hungarians spoke German was as amusing to the Viennese as Irish is to the English and Scottish to the Americans. The Viennese called the Hungarian capital 'Budapest' with only a slight inflection for the Hungarians pronounce it 'Buda-pesht', and they did not take umbrage at the Hungarians calling Vienna 'Bécs'. So there was much 'togetherness' in all this 'doubleness'.

However, if this was true of Vienna it was not true of other 'crown lands'. The Czechs in particular felt much aggrieved. They, too, had been clamouring for home rule and the Hungarian 'Settlement' raised their hopes; but not for long. For the Hungarians would not have their singular position watered down by allowing others to become their equals. The 'Settlement' had left it to personalitities rather than legalities as to who would exercise the greater influence on whom. And there the Hungarians had the upper hand as might have been foreseen. They blocked every attempt at federalization on the Austrian side and in this the emperor's entire sympathies were with them. And so post-war historians came to regard the seemingly happy event of the Hungarian 'Settlement' as one of the many nails in the coffin of the Double Monarchy.

2

The Hungarians

At school we did not learn Hungarian but we had to learn as much about the Hungarians as was to their advantage. The textbooks told us of the defeat at Augsburg, but while they played it down as an ordinary defeat such as could happen to any army, they were rather reticent about the reasons. However, what we learned was enough to make us rather curious to meet Hungarians. They did not come as frequently to Prague as the Viennese did. So I was full of expectations when, around 1910, we set out for Budapest.

From all I heard and read much later I gather that Budapest was not particularly illuminating for anyone who wanted to make the acquaintance of true Hungarians. I remember a certain disappointment: their strange language apart, people generally did not look much different from people in Vienna or Prague. Continentals are, physiognomically, not as uniform as the insular British or the peninsular Spaniards. So one is not surprised to see upturned or downturned noses, high cheek bones, round heads and egg heads, fair hair or dark hair, blue eyes or brown eyes. It is the language rather than the features which unite or divide the races in this Eastern European melting pot. But everywhere, in restaurants and cafés and hotels, there were gipsy bands playing. They were not yet as extravagantly dressed up as they are today, but they wore a kind of national costume, white shirts embroidered with red and black ornaments, jackets with wide sleeves, close-fitting braided trousers and black boots. They were very handsome, dark-skinned with pitch-black shiny hair and moustaches and black eyes, and some sported a golden earring like Captain Morgan. They played, or rather improvised, what everybody believed to be typically and exclusively Hungarian music, the 'primas', or leader, with his violin mysteriously guiding his band which took up his tune, tempo and rhythm even when he walked from table to table playing a languid 'lassu' into the ears of a girl and her boy friend or a fiery 'friss' to awaken a sleepy elderly couple. But most exciting among the players was the man at the ever-present 'cimbalom', a large zither placed on a table and played with two sticks with soft pads at the ends and played, moreover, with incredible virtuosity. The 'cimbalom' is not an instrument of even harmony. It is the wind rustling in the grass of the steppe, the wind of another world, strange, exotic, like the black-haired man who made his two sticks dance on the strings like will-o'-the-wisps so that sometimes it looked as if there were twenty.

This, I thought, was the real Hungary, these were the Hungarians, descendants of the wild horsemen of old. There were more gipsies in Hungary than in any other land of the empire or in any other country in Europe. They were not spoken of as outcasts or layabouts although they had no regular way of life, bred horses and roamed the country. But it all fitted the romantic picture of the old Magyars. And it was all wrong. All the romance was deliberately destroyed. The gipsies, it was said, were not the true Magyars, but the same mysterious race as is found in Spain. And their music is as little Hungarian as Bizet's *Carmen* is Spanish. We were sadly misled, misled by Johann Strauss's *Gipsy Baron*, by Lehár's *Gipsy Love*, by Kalmán's *Gipsy Primas*, by Liszt's 'Hungarian Rhapsodies' and Brahms's 'Hungarian Dances' which should properly be called 'Gipsy Dances'.

Fortunately, when I first went to Budapest people were not so particular about their ancestry and nobody then spoiled my excitement at having come face to face with the native sons of Asia and having felt the wind of the endless steppe in their melancholy or fiery tunes and caught a glimpse of romance in their dark, glowing eyes.

But the true Hungarians, no less than the pseudo-Hungarian gipsies, had a reputation of being romantics and eccentrics, especially the 'magnates', the nobility of old, members of the House of Magnates, owners of two-thirds of the whole country, very wealthy, very picturesque in their old costumes which they wore on state occasions, with fur-trimmed velvet coats and hats and scimitars of Turkish or more ancient Asiatic design. Their portraits in the 'Konditorei Ruszwurm' in Buda showed them as they must have appeared to Abdurrahman Ali, the last Turkish Pasha who lies buried in the fortress of Buda nearby. Hungarians like to tell stories of some of them, of Nicholas Zrinyi who, defending a little fortress with a handful of men against a whole Turkish army, stuffed his pockets with gold ducats before making a last desperate sortie so that the pagans finding his body on the battlefield should not think he was some impecunious nobody; or the story of the hussar general Count Hadik who in 'King' Maria Theresa's day rode with his hussars behind the Prussians' backs all the way to Berlin and returned with a ransom of 300,000 guilders for the 'king's' empty treasury; or the more recent story of Prince Grassalkovitch who managed to squander an enormous fortune in a few years and so brought his palaces in Pressburg (Pozsony-Bratislava) and in Gödöllö into the ownership of the royal house. And it may be recalled that it was one of the wealthiest magnates of the country, Count Michael Károlyi, who was the first—and left-wing socialist—prime minister of the Hungarian republic after the First World War.

But there were other romantics—young Petöfi, the poet and martyr, and Kossuth, the political leader of the 1848 revolution —who believed, as St Stephen had believed 848 years before, that all power, title and dignity of a Hungarian king came not from the Lord or from the people, but emanated from the magic of the golden, jewelled crown. So when Kossuth fled before the advancing Russians and Austrians he took that fetish with him and buried it in Hungarian soil near the Danube before giving himself up to the Turks, convinced that it was the best way of preventing the Habsburgs from ruling in Hungary. Unfortunately the days of fetishes had passed and Emperor Franz Joseph was not unduly worried about the loss of the crown. But when, four years later, the crown was found in a wooden case nine feet deep in the ground, bright and shining as if it had been lying in the treasure house in Buda, he paid due respect to it and had a chapel erected on the spot.

3

The Western 'Orient'

Small nations have their particular problems, especially when they are as different from their neighbours as the Hungarians. These problems are cultural, national, political. Should they isolate themselves? Should they adapt themselves to foreign influences? How can they keep up with their bigger neighbours and still remain themselves? No matter how wise their leaders, it is the character and temperament of the individual alone which decides whether a proper balance can be struck.

The Hungarians solved these problems with commendable ease. They never seem to have suffered from the oppressive feeling that they were too small a nation to survive—something, for instance, which had so often worried the Czechs. They had to learn from their neighbours, but knew how to keep their teachers at arm's length. Their French, Bohemian and Polish kings could not speak their language, but their language proved inextinguishable, even when they introduced Latin as the medium of the courts of justice, of parliament and the administration. But their long familiarity with Latin may have created their enjoyment of the humanities and of learning generally. They were indeed avid learners and, in my time, among the most highly educated people in Europe. In the towns everybody could speak German, from the prime minister down to the cab driver. Hungarians studied abroad, not in Vienna if they could help it because they felt that Vienna could not offer what Budapest did not possess, but in Paris, Zürich or Berlin. They had an extraordinary facility for learning languages which they spoke always with an indelible accent, but otherwise to perfection. From time immemorial there had been a strong Jewish element in Hungary. Some historians believe that there were Jews living among the Magyars as early as the eighth century A.D. when the Magyars still dwelt somewhere between the Black and Caspian Seas. The Jews were happier in Hungary than in any other country of the diaspora. Apart from their religion they were completely 'magyarized' and were leaders in education and learning. The *Pester Lloyd*, a German newspaper published in Budapest, was one of the most respected newspapers in the old Monarchy and Hungary's most important link with the outside world.

The Hungarians had their poets, quite apart from Petöfi. But poetry is hard to translate and to 'internationalize'. Every educated Englishman knows the name of Goethe and every educated German knows the name of Lord Byron, but neither knows much more. Hungarian being so outlandish a language, it is no reflection on the quality of their poetry that names like Petöfi, Vörösmárty, Arány and perhaps a dozen more remain virtually unknown, although it may be said with some justification that there was no Goethe or Lord Byron among them. But there was a novelist, Maurus Jókai, whose novels were still best-sellers in my time and were translated into all European languages. And other new talents were emerging, among them the dramatist Franz Molnar.

Budapest was not, of course, the only town in Hungary. But Hungarian country towns were very different not only from Budapest but from country towns in the Austrian 'crown lands'. I remember a visit to Nagy Kanizsa, a country town in Western Hungary, not far from the Austrian border. It had then only one main street with 'town' houses, very wide and unpaved. In the evening and morning cows and goats were driven through that street to their pastures and the town was lost in the countryside. And the Hungarian countryside was very different from the towns. Hungarian peasants were small-holders or simply farm labourers on the estates of the magnates, and poverty and illiteracy were widespread among them. But there were no beggars. Even the poor and illiterate had their pride, their dignity and their music, later so meticulously collected and written down by Bartók and Kodály.

Budapest competed with Vienna in many ways, but it could not aspire to an equal musical reputation. Certainly Franz Liszt, outmoded today, was then still much appreciated. Piano virtuosos could not do without his 'Années de Pélerinage' or

'Études d'exécution transcendantes', orchestras played his symphonic poems, choirs sang his oratorio *Saint Elizabeth*. Liszt was to the Hungarians what Beethoven was to the Viennese. But, inspired perhaps by the gipsy fiddlers, Hungarians had a knack for the violin and Jenö Hubay was then one of the most famous virtuosos. But Hungarian composers of operettas had to come to Vienna to start a career. Success in Budapest alone was no passport to international fame.

So the strange people from the East who once upon a time had made Europe tremble had at last found their proper place in the European family. There was no sign of the savage past and if the gipsies were not genuine Hungarians one could still see in Budapest or even in Vienna a housemaid or a waiter as dark-skinned and black-haired as a gipsy with a faint hint at slanting eyes—black eyes, of course—who may have preserved some characteristics of the old Magyars. And this type may not have been rare in the solitude of the 'Alföld', the steppe between the Danube and the Tisza which may be similar to their original far-away home.

In Austria and perhaps further afield Hungarians had a reputation of being very clever—and even a little more than clever. In any deal, whether business or politics, a Hungarian always seemed to be one jump ahead of his partner. And Austrian politicians had experienced it often enough. After all, the Balkans, where cleverness and honesty appeared to be irreconcilable, were not far away. One would be wrong to blame it all on the Balkan people. The experience of Turkish administration was not easily forgotten and the Hungarians had had their full share of it. Corruption was said to be the essence of life in Rumania, Serbia or Bulgaria, but one would have hesitated to give so ungracious a name to Hungarian practices. The creaking machinery of state had to be helped and a proper present at the right moment and in the right place did not deserve the name of bribery. Apart from a few innate peculiarities, Hungarians fitted well into European ways and the European spirit, that mixture of tradition and progress which distinguished Europe from the Far East and the Far West and which seems to have faltered only in our day. This spirit made of them lawyers and doctors (and one doctor in particular, Hungarian in spite of his German name Semmelweiss, became a benefactor of mankind when he discovered the causes of puerperal fever), poets and businessmen, philosophers and peasants and growers of the heavy, sweet 'Tokaj' wine, old Emperor Franz Joseph's only companion at meals. But Europe did not spoil their inborn temperament, their language and their character. They were indeed a solid bridge between Europe and the Orient and one felt this very strongly in Budapest where the two worlds met. It was a little miracle that this small nation, wedged between those two worlds, could have held its own through all the vicissitudes of its past. But one only had to look at the Christian names on shops and in the newspapers to see the extraordinary power of assimilation the small nation possessed. Most of the names were 'magyarized' from the catholic calendar, Ferenc for Francis, Lájos for Louis, János for John, Erszébeth for Elizabeth. But one also came across stranger names which could be found in no Roman calendar such as Aladar, Béla, Géza, Zoltán, Sarolta, names from the riding and raiding days which, below the surface of European thinking, living and working, coloured the background of the kingdom of Hungary.

4

The Scent of Paprika

When I first went to Budapest the royal capital, like the imperial capital of Vienna, was at its best. The twin towns of Buda and Pest had been united, the old glory on the right and the smart upstart on the left bank of the Danube which drives majestically right through the city. I remember Buda better than Pest for there were the relics of a romantic past, narrow, cobbled streets climbing up to the fortress which in appearance was more functional than fortresses farther to the West, where military architects had some aesthetic obligations. That fortress of Buda was rather forbidding and its only ornaments, or the ones which impressed me most, were nicely constructed pyramids of cannon balls, some of which had been fired by the Turks at the Austrians, and some by the Austrians at the Turks, and others again by the Austrians at the Hungarians. Nor was the sombre St Matthew's Church nearby inviting, the coronation church of Hungarian kings with the banners of all the Hungarian counties or 'comitats' hung under the gothic vaults and lost in the darkness of the place. It was all a little strange, a little exotic, not quite Western, and not quite Eastern either. There was a royal palace, more modest than the Hofburg in Vienna, much smaller than the castle in Prague, but it was then inhabited by Archduke Joseph, the 'palatine' or king's lieutenant in Hungary and a very popular figure in public life, a 'Hungarian' Habsburg which was no longer a contradiction in terms.

I also remember Elizabeth Bridge, a suspension bridge across the Danube. In Prague we, too, had a suspension bridge which was also called Elizabeth Bridge. But the Danube being twice as wide as the Vltava, the Budapest bridge was regarded in the Monarchy as a great engineering feat and one felt it swinging gently under the heavy traffic. In Pest there were elegant streets; no Ringstrasse, but the straight and exclusive-looking Andrássy Street and Váci Street, with smart shops all built after the 'Settlement' and the last word in European town planning. The large parliament building facing the river had taken its cue from the Palace of Westminster but there, too, was a hint of the Orient which made it look more different than it really was.

There were more cafés in Budapest than in Vienna and more people in the cafés. In Vienna you could spend a few hours in a café. In Budapest you could live there. People were louder, the whole town noisier than Vienna, trams clanged and coachmen shouted. It was another tempo and temperament. People said that Budapest was much naughtier than Vienna, a little Paris of the East where you could make or lose a fortune in the 'Etablissement' on Margaret Island in the Danube between Buda and Pest.

Whether Hungarian cuisine was as old as its practitioners is uncertain. But Hungarian food, like the Hungarians themselves, has a touch of the exotic. One of its products has fought its way into the menus of the world: 'gulash', or, correctly spelt, 'gulyás'. But what was, and still is, served as gulash outside Hungary, even in neighbouring Vienna, is only a rough approximation of the genuine Hungarian dish. Its most important and distinguishing ingredient is red pepper, 'paprika', and nowhere is paprika used more copiously and to greater advantage than in Hungary. Paprika is a variety of Italian peperoni but it has long, thin, red fruits which can be seen strung up under the eaves of Hungarian peasant houses to dry in the September sun. When dry it is ground to a fine red powder. Proper Hungarian gulash is a sea of paprika sauce and the cubes of meat in the sauce are purely ancillary. Nor is there one single or particular type of gulash but a whole range; beef, veal, pork, 'székely' where sauerkraut is married with cubes of pork and paprika sauce. Nor is gulash the only paprika dish of Hungarian cooking. There were 'paprika schnitzel', 'paprika chicken', 'paprika steak', and the paprika sauce was often thickened with cream. Indeed, the sweet, sharp scent of paprika was as peculiar to the atmosphere of Budapest as the scent of 'Gauloises' was to Paris.

Hungary was an agricultural country. It supplied the gourmets in Vienna with the fattest pigs, geese and ducks and the whole Monarchy with the finest flour, 'Hungarian double zero', which was the dream of every good housewife and the basis of all the sweet dishes which Hungarian cuisine produced with a virtuosity only equalled, but not surpassed, by Demel in Vienna. There was indeed a very famous 'Konditorei' in Budapest which we did not miss: Kugler-Gerbaud, Kugler for short, originally Swiss like Caflisch in Naples, but quite magyarized. I remember the red velvet chairs and the mirrors on the walls and the 'Stephanie Torte' and the 'Eszterházy slices' and the 'Kugler Bonbons' which you could even buy in Prague.

Hungarians were not simply proud of Budapest. They were in love with their capital, with their language, with gipsy bands —and with paprika. And the 'Settlement' gave them the uninhibited happiness which was their greatest gift.

5

'A Small Country'

There was, however, one basic error in that 'Settlement'. It made the Hungarians believe that they could govern their destinies themselves. Foreign affairs, the bulk of the army and a large area of finance were 'imperial *and* royal', common to both Austria and Hungary. However strong Hungarian influence was, however much Hungarian assertiveness weighed upon the decisions made in Vienna, Hungary was inescapably caught up in the Austrian net. When the moment of truth came, Hungary had to share the fate of Austria. As elsewhere in the old empire the abandoned gravitational force of the Danube Basin took its revenge beyond the river Leitha and the Hungarians found themselves reduced to the land they had found empty and which they had occupied a thousand years before. When I went to Budapest two years ago the gipsy bands still played and there was no shortage of paprika. But the streets at night were dark and empty, the plaster of the once elegant houses in former Andrássy Street was peeling off. 'We are a small country', an old friend said to me. 'The other day I complained to the municipal office which now owns my house that the rain was coming through the roof. "What can you expect?", the official replied. "We are a small country."'

PRAGUE AND THE CZECHS

I

A Faraway Country

Among the Austrian provinces which turned their back on the Danube and Vienna—and even more so on Budapest—Bohemia was the most important for a variety of reasons: it was the most industrious, the most prosperous and the most rebellious of all the 'crown lands'.

After the First World War a cartoon appeared in Czech newspapers. It showed President Wilson sitting in front of a map of Bohemia, his head buried in his hands, crying: 'I can't find Litomyšl!' Who could have blamed him? To the world at large Prague, Bohemia and all its inhabitants were Austrians, and Austria was represented by Vienna. Vienna overshadowed all the Austrian provinces and none more than Bohemia and Prague. One knew that there were Flemings in Belgium and Basques in Spain, but Czechs in Austria remained anonymous and unremarked.

The reasons are not difficult to see. People have a claim to international attention either if they make a significant contribution to science, literature and the arts or if they are difficult to reach. Unfortunately, none of this applied to the Czechs. As we shall see, they had been struck off the list of European nations for two hundred years and it took another hundred years for them to rise again from oblivion. At the end of the nineteenth century their scientific, literary and artistic achievements were modest, their intellectual life was young, its direction uncertain. Only Czech music had survived all the misfortunes of the nation. Two centuries before Smetana and Dvořák, Czech, like Italian, musicians were found all over Europe. But they seem to have been rather reticent about their homeland and their stock. They were no ambassadors of their people and nobody appeared to care where they came from. Yet it is worth noting that in the middle of the nineteenth century many a gifted young Czech went to Vienna and became Viennese. The so-called 'second flowering' of the Viennese medical school was due to two Czech doctors who became world-famous. But, it could be argued, they were no longer Czechs.

Nor are there any jungles or deserts or strange rites in Bohemia to attract travellers and ethnologists. Even in the eighteenth century it was easier to get into Bohemia than to cross the Alps. But few foreigners came, so that the new Czech intelligentsia in the middle of the last century felt lonely and forgotten. If, in spite of this, a foreigner now and then showed some interest in the country, the Czechs felt personally honoured and were touchingly grateful. In the middle of the nineteenth century a French geologist strayed as far as Prague and found in a rock south of the city the most perfect belemnites. The rock was thereafter called 'Barrand Rock' and when, after the First World War, the Czechs really became affluent and villas, film studios, hotels and restaurants sprang up on and around the rock, the new suburb was named 'Barrandov'. There is no place in France where M. Barrand is so commemorated.

Similarly, and perhaps at M. Barrand's instigation, a French historian, Ernest Denis, came to Prague to study the history of this forgotten people and produced a work in French. It was no best-seller but a railway station and a square were duly named after him.

This kind of recognition made the Czechs believe that they were not as lonely in the world as in fact they were; and that particularly in France they had many friends who understood and appreciated them.

Are the Czechs then a nation without talent except their gift for music? I am biased in their favour. I was born among them, Czech was the first language I spoke, Prague the first sight I saw. A man's birthplace, I believe, is one of the forces which shape his character. It is often the unconscious background to his thinking and feeling, it makes a romantic, a lover of nature, a seeker of pleasures, a planner of great designs. In the difference between a Roman and a New Yorker lies hidden the difference between Rome and New York. At the end of the last century Prague certainly bred romantics, and the Czech people are part of my romantic youth. The Czechs, like any other people, have

96

their faults and their virtues and both have often been exaggerated. If the Czechs were and still are lonely, if their history is a tale of woe rather than of glory and achievement they must, at least to some extent, be answerable for their misfortunes. But that they still exist is a virtue no less remarkable.

2

The City of a Hundred Towers

At the turn of this century Prague had quite a few flattering attributes, both official and unofficial. Officially it was called a 'Royal Capital City'. It was written large above the entrance to the gothic Old Town Hall, on municipal posters, on the tramways—horse-drawn in my early days—nicely arranged round the city's coat of arms: three wedge-shaped towers above a latticed gateway guarded by a mailed fist holding a sword—a little grandiloquent but, alas, the memory of a splendid past rather than a symbol of the modest present.

Unofficially, that is to say, popularly, Prague was called 'Golden Prague' and the 'City of a Hundred Towers'. 'Golden' it certainly was to the Czechs who loved it with a somewhat ostentatious and nervous love, as if suspecting or anticipating contradiction. But Prague was so lovely that any ordinary affection would have been enough. However, if 'golden' may have seemed to some an exaggeration, the hundred towers were not. In fact, statisticians would say that there were more than four hundred. For its size Prague certainly had a disproportionate number of towers, both sacred and profane; very old squat towers, very high gothic towers, those wedge-shaped towers that are shown in the coat of arms, baroque towers with patina-green roofs. The Germans in Prague, no less than the Czechs, knew those towers by name and were proud of every one.

But with all its dusty and paled splendour Prague, the third largest city in the Monarchy, was no more than a provincial town. Vienna, the imperial residence, which set the example for Galician Lemberg no less than for Hungarian Budapest and Croat Agram, was for Prague neither myth nor model. The Habsburgs neglected it. It was their practice to allot an archduke to the more important nations of their empire. There was always a 'Hungarian' archduke residing in Budapest, a 'Polish' archduke living in Cracow, speaking Hungarian and Polish respectively. But there was no 'Czech' archduke, although the heir to the throne, Archduke Franz Ferdinand, married the daughter of a Czech noble family and had his private residence in Bohemia. None of the glory of the imperial court reached Bohemia and Prague and the Czechs tried to take as little notice of Vienna as Vienna took of them. Czech papers never reported the movements of His Imperial Majesty or the dresses of arch-duchesses at public functions and I remember only one visit by Emperor Franz Joseph when he came for a military parade and, without the usual triumphal drive through the town, left barely twenty-four hours after he had arrived.

The world was not quite as peaceful as it now seems to us in retrospect. There was war in South Africa, and in Friedmann's coffee shop on the 'Brückl' where once upon a time a bridge crossed the moat, a highly coloured card was enclosed with every packet of ground coffee showing a battle between the British in red coats and white sun helmets and Boers in broad-brimmed hats and civilian clothes. Pro-Kruger propaganda reached Prague, but as it came from across the German border it was discredited from the start and we all preferred the British.

It was different with the Russian-Japanese war which affected the Czechs more closely because of their sympathies for their fellow-Slavs. A mocking ditty about the Japanese general Kanimura was sung by old and young when he laid siege to Port Arthur. But when the fortress was stormed by the Japanese the Czechs were as crestfallen as if they had lost the war themselves.

These were but flickers of lightning on a distant horizon. In no way was Prague in the main stream of world events. In the window of the clockmaker Hainz in the Old Town Square there was a large clock displaying the time in London, Paris, New York and St Petersburg, and the wide world presented itself to us children in the simple thought that somewhere there were people who had not yet had their breakfast or were just ready to go to bed while we were late for lunch.

3

Vltava

Prague or, as it was officially called, 'Prag', is the Germanized version of its true Czech name 'Praha', the only name used since October 28, 1918. And 'Praha' is derived from the Slav word 'práh',' the threshold', meaning 'the dwelling on the threshold'. It is difficult to see why, in a mythological past, it should have been so called for it is situated on no visible threshold. In fact, the oldest settlement was not called Prague at all but 'Vyšehrad', 'the high castle', not far upstream from present-day Prague; yet only a corner of a wall and the stump of a tower remain, enough to inspire Smetana to a symphonic poem, but not enough to warrant the climb up a slippery slope. Prague itself, of conjectural age, is as much in the centre of Bohemia as the geography of the country would allow.

Today, Prague is the capital of a state which stretches far to the East and calls itself Czechoslovakia. But at the beginning of this century the term 'Czechoslovak' had not yet been invented. Slovakia as such did not exist and I must confess that, at least at school, we were unaware of a Slovak nation, language or literature. Prague was no more than the provincial capital of the 'crown land' Bohemia, then still called a kingdom. The other 'crown lands' which today form the Czechoslovak Republic were the 'margravate' of Moravia and the 'dukedom' of Silesia. They had their own capitals, their own problems and their own interests. If one thought of Prague, one thought of Bohemia alone.

Bohemia is a conspicuous feature of the European map and can be picked out a glance: a more or less quadrilateral standing on one corner, its sides clearly marked by mountain ranges only one of which, the Sudeten, stretching from the Northern to the Eastern corner, passed into international currency when the whole of Northern Bohemia became known as 'Sudetenland'. These Sudeten or 'Giants' Mountains' were then, more innocently, the haunt of the giant 'Rübezahl', pictured with flowing hair and beard, brandishing an enormous staff, frightening lonely wanderers, howling with the snowstorms in winter, helping good and teasing bad people, a rough but kindly spirit of German invention and nationality.

Separating Bohemia from Moravia in the East are the 'Bohemian-Moravian Heights', not much more than a high plateau, but exposed to the cold easterly winds which as late as May can drive snow through the woods and villages while the low-lying country to the West and East basks in the sunshine of spring.

From the Northern to the Western corner there runs the chain of the Erzgebirge or 'Ore Mountains' and that part was better known to the outside world than the rest of Bohemia. There, deep in the woods, are the famous Bohemian spas, hot springs of various temperatures and application: Carlsbad, where millions of sufferers from digestive troubles drank from the 'Sprudel' and ate the delicious wafers called 'Carlsbader Oblaten'; Marienbad, where the corpulent tried to lose some of their excess weight, among them King Edward VII, whose monument was removed only when the communists took over in 1948; Franzensbad, where heart diseases were cured. Many other famous visitors came to these spas, Goethe, Beethoven, the Grand Duke of Weimar, Maharajahs, American millionaires, Balkan potentates, the wonder rabbi of Sadagora, and even Karl Marx. In the days when travelling was the privilege of the few and not the disease of the many, these Bohemian spas with their luxury hotels, their colonnades and 'Kur' parks, 'Kur' promenades and 'Kur' music were indeed the rendezvous of the titled, the rich and the not-too-seriously sick.

And finally, along the Bavarian border in the South-West runs the Böhmerwald, the proverbial 'Bohemian Woods', primeval and, except by one road and railway, never penetrated by man. They are the scene of Schiller's *Die Räuber*, of disinherited nobles turned robbers, and of Weber's *Freischütz*.

Although not very high—the summits rounded by weather and water nowhere reach beyond 4,800 feet—these mountain chains formed an effective barrier and were, at the beginning of the century, still thickly wooded. Mile upon mile of fir and pine covered the slopes and reached far into the plains of the interior.

And somewhere between the rocks and woods in the South-West is the source of the Vltava, or Moldau as it was then generally known, the Vltava of Smetana's tone-poem, the national river of the Czech people and a symbol of their misfortunes. It winds its way through gorges and rapids and then resolutely turns north through open, gently rolling country where every square inch is cultivated, where there is no grass land left for cattle and sheep but field adjoining field, orchard adjoining orchard, and little villages of thatched houses gathered round church and pond, with no hedges obstructing the wide view of fields and sky, the rural idyll of peasant boys and girls dancing polkas and furiants as Smetana has described it in his other tone-poem, 'From Bohemia's Woods and Fields'. And so the river reaches Prague which it divides into two unequal halves.

There Smetana's hymn to the Vltava stops, but the river flows on to its confluence with the Elbe which is a larger stream of lesser repute, at least in Bohemia. For the Elbe only skirts the North-Eastern corner of the country and, after irreverently swallowing the Vltava, leaves it without much further ado, driving a hole through the mountain wall and becoming mighty and powerful—and German. Its name has an evil ring for all the northern Slavs, for the Elbe not only barred their way westward, but they were driven from its banks by German expansion. So the Czechs, last survivors of the 'Elbe Slavs', like to think that without their Vltava the Elbe would not be what it is and scorn the idea that their national river is but a tributary of its bigger, unfriendly sister. However, Prague certainly would not be what it is without the Vltava which in the city is as wide as the Thames at Westminster.

4

Czechs—Bohemians—
'Bohemians'

What could be more natural than that Bohemia should be inhabited by Bohemians, as Britain is inhabited by the British, and France by the French? But the case of Bohemia is infinitely complicated.

The name itself is wrong. Once upon a time Bohemia was inhabited by the 'Boii', a Celtic people presumably, mentioned by Julius Caesar, but long since lost without a trace except for the name which inexplicably stuck to the country for more than two thousand years.

And the Bohemians—totally unrelated to Caesar's 'Boii'—present an unusual problem. For reasons unexplained certain people are called 'Bohemians', although they have no connection with Bohemia. They are mentioned by Henri Murger in the middle of the nineteenth century and were introduced by him into the realms of world literature. But he did not discover them. He complains that before him those 'Bohemians' had been shamefully misrepresented by certain boulevard dramatists as 'saltimbanques', bear-leaders and fire-eaters, people whose profession and purpose in life was to have neither. Murger having studied the subject more closely assures his readers that the 'Bohemians' are, in fact, artists, poets, musicians not yet and perhaps never to be recognized, devotees of the muses, insensitive to worldly rewards, warm hearts in cold attics, a brotherhood of rich imagination in poor attire, and domiciled in Paris as might be expected. In short, the characters of Puccini's opera.

The *Oxford Dictionary*, more succinctly, describes 'Bohemians' as 'socially unconventional people'. Others, more realistic and less fanciful, have suggested that the genuine 'Bohemians' were not artists in any sense but vagrant tinkers. It is true that the 'dráteník', the man, or sometimes boy, with an assortment of wires slung round his shoulder, a pair of pliers in his hand and a friendly smile on his face, was in my time a familiar figure not only in Prague but in towns and villages all over Bohemia and perhaps beyond, mending broken pots and jars by wiring the pieces together, always welcome, for in those thrifty days the good housewife did not lightly throw away what could be mended.

So much for the romantic view. The truth is otherwise. The genuine Bohemians, inhabitants of Bohemia, are neither unsuccessful artists nor socially unconventional people and the percentage of tinkers was even in the old days quite insignificant. The inhabitants of Bohemia were quite ordinary, conventional people of all trades and professions. However, there were until the more recent upheavals two different types of 'Bohemians' in Bohemia; the Germans who called themselves 'Bohemians' and the country 'Bohemia', and the Czechs who called themselves 'Czechs' and the country 'Čechy'. And the two disagreed with each other on a great many other matters.

5

Uneasy Bedfellows

Knowledge of the Czechs is rather superficial. They are Slavs, and another glance at the map will show that they are the westernmost Slavs. Their appearance is unmistakably Slav: men and women are rather stocky with broad faces and high cheekbones. The thin, lanky type of Masaryk is an exception. Think rather of Smetana and Dvořák. They are jovial by nature, they like a good joke and their language lends itself easily to jokes.

That language has, of course, its family likeness with other Slav languages, but it is not simply a dialect of any of them but a language of its own. Strangely enough the Czech language, though more directly exposed to foreign and especially German influence, is purer than the others. There are words in daily use which in other Slav languages are 'glagolitic', the old Slav vernacular of the church. In their isolation from other Slavs the same may have happened to the Czechs as happened to the Spanish in South America or to the French in Canada who preserved in their speech a flavour of antiquity. I admire the language, not because it was my first language, but because it is in its own way ingenious. For a philologist it could easily be what a botanical garden is for the botanist. It has a wildly complicated grammar which is difficult to learn, but instinctively applied by both the learned and the ordinary folk: declension with six cases and three genders differentiates between animate and inanimate objects and between the consonants at the end of the root-syllable which may be soft, medium or hard; it has a wealth of verbal forms such as iteratives and duratives which enable one to say in two words what in any other language requires a whole sentence, such as 'Jda čtu'—'I read while I am walking'.

But to those who do not understand it, Czech is not a melodious language like French, Italian or Spanish. It sounds harder than any other Slav language and manages to get by with very few vowels. There was a tongue-twister we used as children because of its curious absence of all vowels: 'Strč prst skrz krk'—'put a finger through the throat', But, at least for the Czechs themselves, it is a most singable language as not only Smetana demonstrated. When I was a child the whole town of Prague and the whole countryside was full of song.

For some reason, in foreign performances of *The Bartered Bride*, one often sees Czech peasants in Hungarian costumes such as have become familiar through Hungarian gipsy bands all over the world. I can assure the reader that the Czechs have nothing in common with the Hungarians except a mutual dislike of each other. Their origin, their language, their costumes and customs are totally different.

So much for the Czechs in 'Čechy'. But there were also the German Bohemians in Bohemia, a minority of one-third of the total population scattered in and around the towns of the interior, but living all along the borders of Prussian Silesia, Saxony and Bavaria in 'their' territory which was as if cut out of the country with a sharp knife. As a schoolboy I spent a few summers in a village in Northern Bohemia called Hirschberg. It had no Czech name and was just inside 'German territory'. Nobody there spoke or understood Czech. But hardly two miles away, across the invisible and unmarked 'language frontier', was the village of Bezděz, dominated by the remains of a mediaeval castle, where all the villagers had Czech names, spoke only Czech and did not understand one word of German.

This German 'Northern Bohemia' as it was inaccurately called (for the German territory included also the South-West of the country with its mountains and forests) was not as fertile as the Czech interior and, therefore, less agricultural, but industrialized and highly prosperous. The paper mills of Hohenelbe supplied half the cigarette paper of the world, the coloured glass beads round the necks of African chiefs and also the finest cut glass came from the glass works in and around Gablonz, Bohemian porcelain from Schlaggenwald graced princely tables, uranium was mined in Joachimsthal, and from the Adriatic to the Vistula the imperial-royal state railways puffed smoke from the soft coal dug up in Brüx and Dux. The towns were more sophisticated and elegant than Czech towns and German Reichenberg and Teplitz-Schönau had their municipal theatres playing opera, operetta and drama all the year round. In short, the Germans in Bohemia were a thorn in the side of every Czech man, woman and child.

6

How it came about

It was a misfortune for both that these two nations were thrown so closely together in one country. Everything seemed to conspire to bring it about—history, geography, politics and common greed.

The trouble really began with the isolation of the Czech people from their brethren; in the North by German expansion and in the South by Hungarian invasion. It was then the geography of their country which protected and isolated them. Once the avant-garde of the great Slav migration, they were already in the tenth century A.D. a splinter group surrounded on three sides by Germans. And Germans were never comfortable neighbours, for they had a voracious appetite for land and learning. The dense forests around Bohemia kept their armies at bay but their reputation as scholars reached the rural courts of early Czech kings. So, harmlessly enough, German teachers came, monks, holy men with good intentions. What we know of good King Wenceslas we know from them.

They were, unwittingly, the forerunners of traders whose purpose was less saintly. In Bohemia there was a rural society uncontaminated by money and luxurious living. Such a 'market' always attracted trade and paid good dividends. Bohemian kings were the first to fall for money and luxuries and they welcomed the German traders.

Behind the towering stone mountain of Tyne Church in Prague there still stands a large complex of very old, squat buildings grouped around a vast courtyard, the 'Old Ungelt', the caravanserai of German merchants dating back to the twelfth century, with stables, warehouses, an inn and a brewery. There the goods lay in bond; hence the name 'Ungelt' which means 'duty-free'. The inn and brewery were still flourishing in my time while the bustle of the old market-place had long vanished and carpenters, cabinet-makers and cobblers had established their workshops in the quiet yard.

The traders, no doubt, had tales to tell of German towns and crafts, of castles, gold and silver mines. Czech kings listened and could not resist. They invited German builders, craftsmen and miners, they gave them land and granted privileges and these efficient 'settlers' duly built castles and towns and churches and discovered the rich deposits of gold and silver in the South-West of the country. They filled the kings' treasury while the Czechs tilling their fields and tending their cattle looked on suspiciously. Xenophobia is the burden a splinter nation has to bear, but a wise man might have shown the Czechs how to learn from these clever foreigners. No such wise man was at hand. Nor were the Germans friendly teachers. They were overbearing, did not mix with the Czechs, and kept their knowledge to themselves. However, by the beginning of the thirteenth century the Czech kings were reputed to be the richest in Europe, thanks to the privileged foreigners in their midst.

So the seeds of a conflict were sown which to this day has not been resolved. The Germans had never conquered Bohemia by the sword. They were not guilty of any 'germanization' such as they had practised in Brandenburg and Pomerania. The 'Knights of the German Order', who had massacred tens of thousands of Slavs, left Bohemia alone. But German dominance was of a subtler, more pervasive, more irresistible kind. The Czechs hated the Germans and the Germans knew it. But there was no mediator when mediation could have succeeded. And so Czech history became a tale of woe.

Three tragedies stand like milestones on the road of the Czech people up to the 'Collapse' of the Habsburg empire (a fourth occurred in 1939, a fifth in 1948, and yet a sixth in 1968).

We have already touched upon the first, which began in 1278 with the defeat and death of King Przemysl Otakar II who fell a victim not only to Rudolf of Habsburg's superior power but to a conspiracy of his own noblemen who dreaded a Bohemian empire dominated by a German majority. This tragedy ended twenty-five years later with the murder of the king's grandson, a boy of eighteen, who, in spite of his grandfather's experience, had been brought up as a German. He was the last of the reigning house of the legendary Queen Libussa and her husband Przemysl which had guided the destinies of the Czechs from time immemorial. He was the first prominent and the saddest victim of the 'German Question'. Except for a few years in the late fifteenth century, no Czech was to wear the Bohemian crown again.

The second and larger tragedy began on July 6, 1415, when Jan Hus, a Czech 'magister' of Prague university, was burned at the stake in Constance. I must explain briefly how it came about.

After the violent death of the last of the 'Przemyslides', the Czech nobility could not agree on a king from among themselves and elected Count John of Luxemburg on condition that no foreigner should be given an office of state. John had no difficulty in meeting this condition. He was a brawler in the knightly fashion of the day, spent his time fighting and jousting abroad, and lost his life at Crécy on the side of the French. But his son Charles who followed him in Bohemia and, as Charles IV, was elected king of Germany and emperor of the Holy Roman Empire, brought unprecedented splendour and prosperity to Bohemia and to Prague, now the capital of Central Europe. But it was during his reign that the Bohemian territories 'colonized' by Germans became a country within a country and that more foreigners were invited. A Frenchman began building St Vitus Cathedral (a German completed it), Germans built the stone bridge across the river and the famous Karlstein Castle near Prague. In 1348 King Charles founded in Prague the first university in Central Europe which was at once dominated by German teachers and students. And Charles's daughter Anne married King Richard II of England. That marriage added to the fame of Prague and Bohemia but it did not make the Czechs a famous nation. Charles, 'Bohemia's father', died unaware of any discord among his subjects, but his son was soon to face it. Some of the Bohemians who accompanied Anne to England probably brought back Wyclif's writings and Jan Hus, a Czech peasant's son, priest and 'magister', made them the springboard for his campaign against the Pope, the clergy, and the Germans. Understandably, these happy and prosperous Germans rejected any suggestion of reformation, but the Czechs flocked to hear the thunder of Hus's sermons in Bethlehem Church which still stands, dark and sinister, among the ancient houses of the Old Town. One day, after another wild sermon, the mob invaded the university, the 'Carolinum', killed some of the teachers and students and chased the rest through the streets. Whereupon the Germans packed their belongings, left Prague and prudently founded the university of Leipzig. Hus was summoned to the Church Council in Constance, sentenced as a heretic and, in spite of the king's safe-conduct, was burned at the stake. Thus the scene was set for the second tragedy of the Czech people— and the first of the German 'colonists'.

The Czechs rose in anger at the death of their martyr. A Czech knight invented a new technique of warfare and collected an army—'The Lord's Warriors'—under the white banner with the red chalice of the 'Husites'. The Germans in Prague and in the country who had not fled in time were massacred and the Husite army fell upon the neighbouring German provinces of Saxony, Thuringia, Bavaria and Austria, burning towns and villages and routing the armies sent against them one by one. The 'Husite Storm' lived long in the memory of its survivors and gave the Czechs a bad name.

It was all heroic; and it was all futile. Good King Charles had meant to make Bohemia a paradise on earth, but it had become a hell. The king fled, administration broke down, and the anarchy which followed did not spare the Czechs themselves. After their triumph of revenge the Husites found themselves without purpose or prospects. After twenty years of bloodshed, moderate and radical Husites met in battle. The radicals were beaten, their leader killed, and the moderates sought peace. The king returned to his throne, the Germans to their land and towns, the Czechs to their farmsteads, their name stained and nothing achieved but a measure of religious freedom. The world has never given any credit to Jan Hus or to the Czechs for having introduced and instituted a reformed Christian faith a hundred years before Luther, Calvin and Knox. On the vast Reformation Monument in Geneva there is a great assembly of reformers carved in stone, among them even the totally unknown Transylvanian Stephen Bocskai. But the visitor will look in vain for Jan Hus. Thus ended the second tragedy.

The third and worst began on May 23, 1618, when a group of

Czech noblemen stormed into the office of the two chancellors of the kingdom on the Hradschin in Prague and threw them out of an upper window into the moat of the castle. The noblemen chose this curious method of demonstrating their opposition to the government, now the government of a Habsburg king; for in 1526 the Habsburgs finally established themselves in Bohemia. They refused to tolerate any reformation, Husite or otherwise, and revoked the religious freedom of the Czechs. Hence the celebrated 'Defenestration of Prague'. But the two officials were more fortunate than their assailants, for they landed on a dungheap and miraculously escaped, while those who attempted their execution were themselves executed. The war which followed this tragi-comic incident was decided in one single battle of a few hours at the gates of Prague. The Czechs were beaten by an Austrian army and twenty-eight of their leaders were beheaded in the Old Town Square. This sealed the fate of the Czechs for the next two hundred years. As Czech reformation and nationalism were identical, the Habsburgs felt that they had to suppress both. A 'New Order' was introduced in Bohemia by which not only reformed churches were closed and their preachers evicted, but the Czech language was proscribed, Czech schools banned, the printing of Czech books made a punishable offence. The best men of the nation went into exile, among them Jan Amos Komenský who found asylum in Holland where he published, under his latinized name Comenius, his famous 'Orbis Pictus', the foundation of modern education.

From Bohemia, the ripples spread far and wide. The events of 1618 were the signal for the Thirty Years War, the most devastating war Central Europe had suffered. By a whim of history this war, which swayed from the Baltic to the Alps and from Poland to the Rhine, ended after thirty years precisely where it had started: in Prague. But Prague was no longer a royal residence. The Habsburgs avoided it. The enormous castle on the Hradschin remained empty until the first president of the new Republic moved in three hundred years later. Like all other Bohemian towns, Prague became German and provincial. What was Czech—people and tradition—retreated to the villages, to Smetana's 'Bohemian Woods and Fields', and an illiterate peasantry was the nation's only hope for the future, if indeed any hope was left. The Czechs were completely routed, utterly overwhelmed.

*   *   *

After the First World War a book by a Czech writer became a best-seller all over the world. It was translated into every living language, serialized, dramatized, filmed, even imitated: the story of 'the good soldier Švejk'. Its author, Jaroslav Hašek, was hardly known to the Czechs themselves and died soon after the book was first published and before he could enjoy his own success. Henri Murger would have loved to meet him, for Hašek had everything Murger attributed to his 'Bohemians'. He was a poet, he was poor, he was wayward, and he was a genuine Bohemian. Never before had a Czech writer become so famous, or a Czech character so popular. How 'Czech' the good soldier Švejk was foreign readers little knew. His was the story of a defenceless people under the heel of a hostile régime which could not be outfought, but which *could* be outwitted. Here was a little man of imperturbable good humour in desperate circumstances but with all his desperation hidden behind a sly smile and an easy joke, always doing the wrong thing in pardonable error, a dangerous man, but an accomplished actor, wide-eyed, innocent. In fact, the imperial and royal armies were full of Czech Švejks who misunderstood orders, misdirected troop trains, misconnected telephones, mislaid important mail, misread official war bulletins, without ever openly misbehaving. Readers abroad might have thought that the good soldier Švejk, if not Hašek's invention, was the product of the First World War. But that war only gave him his final professional polish. His virtuosity in cheating the authorities had been gained in two hundred years of bitter experience. The Czechs were determined to survive the disaster of 1621, the year of their defeat, without proclaiming it. For two hundred years Švejk was the unsung hero of their survival, of the art of overcoming all the odds. Jaroslav Hašek might have shared the literary fame of Cervantes and de Coster, Švejk the immortality of Don Quixote and Till Eulenspiegel. But his was not the eternal tragi-comedy of human weaknesses, with all their mirth and melancholy. Don Quixote and Till Eulenspiegel lost in the end, but Švejk won. That was his undoing. After his universal triumph he was soon forgotten. Even the Czechs themselves forgot him. He was no longer at his best when the Germans assumed the 'protection' of the Czechs in 1939; and in 1968, when they might again have needed his slippery humour and his adroit avoidance of submission, he deserted them altogether.

However, if the worldly authorities could be deceived the church could not. By subtler and more expensive means it set out to reconquer the lost ground. The God of counter-reformation was no longer a persecutor or executioner but a God of splendour, of stucco and gold, of jubilating puttoes and ecstatic saints. The Husite spirit of sinister austerity was to be exorcized by pomp and glitter. The most famous German and Italian architects of the time were called to Prague and not only transformed the dark interiors of former Husite churches, but built resplendent new theatres of the faith, St Nicholas on the left and another St Nicholas on the right bank of the Vltava, St James and St Charles. Baroque was the last addition to Prague's architectural fame. This masterful campaign was as successful as the political repression was a failure. When the Czechs reappeared on the scene they were Catholics again and no ill-feelings troubled their devotion to Rome.

7

The Re-awakening

The Czechs, in fact, did reappear decisively on the scene.

When, in 1786, Mozart came to Prague, his friends there with their Czech names, Duschek or Niemetschek spelt in the German way, were to all intents and purposes Germans. But it was at this precise moment that the iron grip of the Viennese government loosened and the nation slowly awoke from its sleep. The Czechs call the following half-century the 'Re-awakening'. To re-awaken a nation of illiterate peasants seemed an impossible task. A man like Franz Niemetschek, Ph.D. who brought up Mozart's sons in Prague would not have known how to spell his name the Czech way. The first generation of 're-awakeners' had to resuscitate the language, its vocabulary, its grammar, its spelling. It took more than thirty years before, in 1835, a Czech-German dictionary could be published with the support of a totally Germanized and Austrianized former Czech nobility. The second generation, still educated in German schools and universities, had to create a literature and a reading public. It was an even harder and more emotional undertaking, and desperate things happened. Two enthusiastic re-awakeners forged allegedly mediaeval manuscripts in an attempt to prove that Czech literature was as old and as good as the German. And finally the Czechs had to be told their forgotten history and František Palacký became their classical historian.

Told thus briefly, the drama of this 'Re-awakening' cannot easily be appreciated; but it was a high drama of hope and illusion which reached far into the villages of the Czech countryside. The re-awakeners were without exception sons of peasants and farm labourers and some of them, when boys, walked barefoot all the way to Vienna to find a place in a grammar school. There, in the heart of Europe, a new nation was born which was a long way behind its fellow-Europeans and was determined to catch up with them. It is worth remembering that at about the same time a similar effort by the 'félibriges', Mistral and Roumanille, in Provence failed, while the Czechs succeeded.

After the revolution of 1848, which affected Prague no less than Vienna, Czech primary and secondary schools were opened again and Prague university was divided into a German and a Czech department. This decisively changed the character of Czech society. There was no longer any need for Czech boys to go to German schools, or to walk barefoot to Vienna. They went to Prague, became doctors, lawyers, shopkeepers, journalists—even journalists, for after sixty years of trial and disappointment a Czech daily paper was at last able to maintain itself. In short, they were urbanized. Smetana, who had followed in the footsteps of earlier Czech musicians and had gone abroad, had, after his return, to conduct his and other operas in the 'temporary theatre', a poor wooden structure. But he lived to see the National Theatre built and ceremonially opened with his festival opera *Libussa*. The National Museum was designed as an impressive backcloth to Wenceslas Square, and a new Czech Prague began to rise, inexorably crowding out the Germans in the town.

It was their historian Palacký who led the Czechs from their past into the present, from history to politics. He turned the 'German question' which weighed upon every Czech's mind into an 'Austrian question'. He had no doubt that the Czechs had to find their proper place in the Monarchy. But the Hungarian Settlement of 1867 split that Monarchy down the middle and left the Austrian half predominantly Slav. Poles, Czechs, Croats, Slovenes and Serbs made up two-thirds of the Austrian population. Therefore, Palacký's political programme was for the federalization of Austria, with home rule for every nation and with the emperor as umpire. This programme was called 'Austro-Slavism' and its promoters came to be known as the 'Old Czechs', gentlemen who assured the emperor of their loyalty, provided that . . .

Palacký's programme was too reasonable to find favour in Vienna. Emperor Franz Joseph, still smarting under the Hungarian Settlement, rejected any further splitting and his German subjects supported him vigorously. At the end of the nineteenth century, when I was a youngster, the 'Old Czechs' and 'Austro-Slavism' were discredited and a younger and less gentlemanly generation, the 'Young Czechs', took their place in politics. They were more self-confident, more vociferous and more radical; and they replaced 'Austro-Slavism' by 'Pan-Slavism'. It so happened that at the same time radicals in Vienna hit upon 'Pan-Germanism', an idea which set in train the ultimate troubles of the Monarchy. From an Austrian point of view, both 'Pan-Slavism' and 'Pan-Germanism' were equally treasonable. But 'Pan-Germanism', or in simpler terms union with the glorious and victorious German Reich, was a real danger, while 'Pan-Slavism', the union of all Slav people, was mere utopia. The Poles in Austria would have no truck with the Russians, the Croats were traditionally the most loyal subjects of the Habsburgs and thought little of the less educated and less prosperous Slovenes and the Slovenes thought nothing of the Serbs. The reader may recall the 'Kingdom SHS' which was established after the 1914–18 war and which united all these Yugoslavs (it was, after all, a Croat who shot a Serbian king). But as a slogan 'Pan-Slavism' was highly attractive. 'Svůj k svému', 'each to his own kith and kin' (notice how short and precise the Czech language can be) was something everybody could understand without having read the eleven volumes of Palacký's *History of the Czech people in Bohemia and Moravia*. The Germans were alarmed. The most famous of living German historians, Theodor Mommsen, called all Germans to arms against the 'Slav apostles of barbarism', while Grand Duke Nikolaj of Russia, later commander-in-chief of the Russian armies in the Great War, came to Prague (though *not* to Vienna), was received by the municipal dignitaries with much pomp and ceremony, and wildly greeted by the populace. Imperial Russian politics never missed an opportunity of embarrassing the Austrian government.

The unfortunate Austrian government was embarrassed enough without Russian diplomacy, not least by the newcomers on the political scene, the Social Democrats. The Czechs, too, had their social democratic party which subscribed to the other simple slogan: 'Workers of the World, unite!', on the understanding, however, that German workers were not included.

One man stood in the shadow of Czech public life: Thomas

Garrigue Masaryk, the son of a coachman on an imperial estate in Moravia, educated in Vienna and Leipzig, married to an improbably poor American girl whose name he added to his, professor of philosophy at the Czech department of Prague university, a man dedicated to honesty but not to politics. He disagreed with the general view that the Germans alone were to blame for the misfortunes of the Czechs. The Czechs, he wrote, had a fatal taste for fighting against impossible odds instead of coming to terms with them, and this made them admirers of martyrs and martyrdom. 'It is easier to die for one's ideals than to live for them', he wrote. All their venerated martyrs, King Przemysl Otakar, Jan Hus, the twenty-eight noblemen, fought for unattainable ideals and died in vain (and that was still true of the young student, Jan Palach, in 1968). The Czechs did not like Masaryk's criticisms. Nor did they like it when he insisted on the removal of the forged 'mediaeval' manuscripts from the National Museum, or when he stood up for a half-witted Jewish man accused of ritual murder, or when he accused Prague municipal councillors of bribery. Nobody would have expected him ever to play any prominent part in politics. But when the Great War broke out he was the only distinguished Czech abroad and he rightly judged that the old Monarchy had no chance of survival. He had always called himself a 'realist', and as a realist he had to provide for Czech existence after the inevitable 'Collapse'. So the stepson became the father of the nation and his moderation was one of the most precious assets of the new Republic, though, alas, a vanishing asset.

As a nation the Czechs had made notable progress. They had built their National Theatre, their National Museum, they had primary and grammar schools and Prague university had been divided into Czech and a German departments. If all this had been granted to them fifty years earlier it might have satisfied them. Now it was not enough. The Germans in Prague were a small minority without representation on the town council. But they had two theatres, a large concert hall, two daily papers, the streets and squares had both German and Czech names. It was a source of profound irritation to the Czechs. The underlying tension affected life in the city and the Germans were in no mood to make themselves invisible. It was inadvisable to speak German in the Café Slavia opposite the National Theatre, but equally unwise to speak Czech in the Café Continental on the Graben. Working days were usually quiet and peaceful enough. Part of the goodness of the 'good old days' must have been the general respect for and enjoyment of work; and everybody worked six full days a week. But Sunday was the day for politics. It began in the morning when the 'colour' students of the German university held their 'corso' on the Graben, marching in long crocodiles up and down wearing their coloured hats. Each 'club' had its own colour and was named after some defunct German tribe, preferably one of those who were thought to have lived in Bohemia before the Czechs arrived, such as 'Rugia' or 'Markomannia'. They all had their secret hide-outs, known only to them and to the police, where they fought their strictly prohibited duels which were not designed to kill a man but only to leave a scar on his face as an indisputable witness to his courage. When they had had their marching exercise they disappeared into the Deutsches Haus for their 'Frühschoppen' or morning drink—there were no licensing hours in Austria— where Herr Zogelmann and his German waiters attended to their needs.

Although it was for them an acquired taste, the Czech students thought they owed it to themselves and to the nation to have their own 'corso', and not too far from the Germans. As they had no romantic background of ancestral tribes and did not wish to imitate the 'colours' of the Germans, they sported black velvet berets of the type worn by the 'bohemians' of Montparnasse. Now and then they strayed to the Graben while the German 'corso' was in full swing and the ensuing shouting match often ended in blows, with the police being accused in the German papers of enjoying the spectacle while the Czech papers complained of German provocation. This was not altogether unwarranted for the German students had the absurd habit of singing 'Die Wacht am Rhein'—'The Watch on The Rhine', whereupon the Czech students naturally felt that they had to defend the honour of the Vltava and replied with their fighting song 'Hej, slované' which, among other things, assured the singers and listeners that the Lord would wipe out all Germans even if there were as many as there are devils in hell.

Such was a Sunday morning on the Graben. The afternoons belonged to the Czechs. From the houses in Wenceslas Square and around hung red and white flags, the national colours, the 'Sokol' held its weekly 'slet' or meeting in para-military uniforms and formations, the streets swarmed with boys and girls, men and women in national costumes. Kmoch's band from Kolin, a country town east of Prague, marched through the streets playing Czech folksongs and marches and a member of parliament named Klofáč made inflammatory speeches. The consumption of beer was phenomenal and the inexperienced observer might well have thought that revolution was round the corner. But it was not. On Monday morning all was quiet again and everybody went to work as if nothing had happened.

Only once did matters seem to get out of hand. In 1908, after thirty years of occupation, Austria annexed the former Turkish provinces of Bosnia and Herzegovina far away on the Adriatic. The kingdom of Serbia reacted violently to this annexation for it had expected to be presented with the provinces which would have given the Serbs access to the sea. Russia, predictably, supported Serbian aspirations. This caused a European crisis and if Russia had not been smarting under its Japanese defeat and the revolution of 1905, it would have gone to war with Austria. But for the chimera of 'Pan-Slavism' this would have been of no concern to the Czechs. However, while the rest of the Monarchy remained calm, Prague and the Czechs exploded into what appeared to be open revolt. I remember how, in the middle of the morning, the director of my school, a bearded, usually expressionless ogre, entered the classroom in a state of high excitement and told us that the school would be closed immediately and until further notice, that we should all go home quietly and singly, avoid all gatherings in the streets, and stay indoors. We did not know what had happened and I still do not know how it all began. In the morning I had gone to school with father as usual and the streets had been as quiet as on any other day. But now when we walked outside, the streets were thronged with chanting and shouting crowds, the police had disappeared, and at the crossing of two main roads a double row of soldiers with fixed bayonets barred the way. As I emerged from one of the many Prague passageways I just missed a squadron of dragoons on horseback with drawn sabres clearing the street of demonstrators. By a wide detour, more excited than frightened, I reached home to the great relief of my parents. In the afternoon at the corner below our windows a platoon of soldiers drew up, a bugle call rang through the deserted street, and a gentleman in a dark suit and bowler hat read the articles of martial law. Revolution! How marvellous, we children thought. But father paced anxiously up and down the room and mother looked worried. Perhaps the future was not as secure as many people believed.

However, a few days later everything returned to normal. Schools and shops opened, the troops were withdrawn, martial law was lifted, and the students resumed their Sunday 'corso'. The papers printed lists of people killed or wounded in the riots on the other side of the river and the re-established calm seemed to prove that in spite of it all Austria would live for ever, as the national anthem complacently assured us.

8

'Kde domov můj?'

In more romantic days and usually under some stress nations found that they needed an outward sign of their nationhood, an expression of their belief in themselves and in their mission to defend themselves, or to subdue others, or both. And so national anthems came into being. Some were written for the purpose, such as Joseph Haydn's Austrian anthem, and others were children of the moment which were found to serve the purpose and, by a tacit consensus of opinion, were raised to the status of *vox populi*. Such were 'God save the Queen' or the 'Marseillaise'. In our time these anthems have been largely emptied of their emotional content and have become no more than a mere identification mark, a badge worn on particular occasions.

And the Czechs too acquired a national anthem which to this day they have kept as a memorial of the first morning of their new national life. Of course, in imperial Austria there was only one official national anthem, Haydn's immortal tune with words adapted so that they did not refer to any particular emperor (as in 1797) but to all future emperors who might stand in need of 'preservation', and explaining why at great length. It was translated into all the eleven languages of the Monarchy and schoolchildren everywhere had to know it by heart. Only Czech children learnt another song as well, their own national anthem which was quite unofficial and unrecognized by the authorities, but not prohibited either for no censor could have found anything in words or music to justify prohibition. Perhaps it was one of pre-war Švejk's jokes with a deeply serious meaning.

It is the most peculiar of all national anthems I know and most characteristic of those who sang it first and are still singing

it today. To begin with, its title is unusual: 'Kde domov můj?',
'Where is my homeland?', a question, where instead one would
expect a firm assertion. Like other songs which were not written
for the purpose, this one was not meant to be or to become a
national anthem. It was composed by an otherwise insignificant
Czech composer for a popular farce by one of the earliest Czech
dramatists and first sung in a makeshift theatre on December 21,
1834. In the play a vagrant tinker boy in a foreign land is asked
where his homeland his and he sadly remembers, repeating the
question: 'Kde domov můj?'. And he goes on to describe it.
'The waters murmur in the fields, the forests rustle on the rocks,
spring blossoms in the woods, a paradise on earth to see—that is
the Czech land, my homeland'—'země česká, domov můj'.
Both words and melody are equally beautiful, equally melancholy, seemingly equally unsuitable for a national anthem.
There is nothing aggressive, nothing haughty, nothing defiant
in it. One cannot march to this slow tune. One has to stand up
to sing it. It does not pretend that the Czechs are the best people,
their country the best country in the world. It does not praise
the national colours or virtues or the glory of military exploits.
It does not pray for anyone to be preserved for the good of the
people or of mankind. The beauty of the country and of spring
of which it tells are in no way singular, for the waters murmur,
forests rustle and spring blossoms wherever there are waters,
forests and spring. It only asserts the simple truth that home is
sweeter than any foreign land, which is as true of the Czechs as
it is of Eskimos or Bedouins. If at the end of the second verse—
and it has only two verses—it goes one small step beyond, it
only unconsciously admits that the Czechs are happy only with
their own kith and kin and unable to mix with others. And this
is the theme of their existence, the root of all the evil that has
befallen them. There, in a few words, lie consolation and con-
demnation close together. The words, no less than the slow
tune, are nostalgic, nothing more; which is quite unique for a
song which should rouse, excite, unite, like the 'Marseillaise', or
the 'Brabançonne', or should be a common prayer like 'God
save the Queen'. That this song was greeted with passionate
enthusiasm in 1834 when the nation had hardly opened its eyes
and looked around for the first time in two hundred years was
understandable enough. But the nation has kept it as its

anthem to this day when the Czechs sing it as they sang it then, the song of a land which seems to be far away, a land which was once theirs and will never be quite theirs again. There is no future, no hope in this strange anthem and the Czechs are still asking the question which, one would have thought, had been answered on October 28, 1918.

So the censor could do nothing about it. Nor could the police, when on summer afternoons in the open-air café-restaurant in the 'stromovka' or 'Tree Garden' the band of Infantry Regiment No. 28 played first the official anthem, which was listened to in sullen silence, and then followed with 'Kde domov můj?' and everybody stood up and clapped frantically. So when the day of liberation came, that October day in 1918, the little song was invested with all the honours of exclusivity and Haydn's tune was left to its fate to be stolen like a jewel from the fallen crown of the Habsburgs and to become 'Deutschland, Deutschland über alles'.

Witnessing from far away the events of the last thirty years I cannot help feeling the tragedy of this handful of lovable people, stranded in the midst of Europe, who will not succumb and cannot succeed.

9

Moravia—Silesia—Slovakia

Masaryk was Moravian and it may be appropriate to look briefly at the other lands which today are part of the Czechoslovak Republic, and at their Austrian past.

Next to Bohemia, Moravia is the most important of them. It once dominated the early history of the Czechs, later became part of the Bohemian kingdom and, since Habsburg days, a margravate of its own, a 'crown land' like all the other provinces of the Monarchy. It was completely different from Bohemia. The country was to all its inhabitants 'Moravia', that is 'Morava' for the Czechs and 'Mähren' for the Germans, and both called themselves Moravians. The Czechs in Moravia were cousins rather than brothers of the Czechs in Bohemia. They spoke a dialect dotted with German words. There were no compact German territories and no 'language frontiers', but, at the beginning of this century, all the towns, large and small, still had sizeable German majorities and German administration and were called 'language islands', for all the countryside around them was Czech of the Moravian variety. The central and South-Eastern parts had the richest soil in the Monarchy— and the richest peasants. The area was called the 'Hana' and its people the 'Hanaks' and it was said that the shiny buttons on their Sunday coats were of pure gold. Worse still from the Czech point of view, they were loyal Austrians and liked the Habsburgs who had large estates in the country. In many cottages, white-washed and with bright blue or red stripes at the base of the walls, there hung a picture of the scene when Emperor Joseph II, who had set them free in 1781, left his coach on seeing a peasant ploughing, took the plough, drew a furrow and told the astonished man: 'From today this field is yours, but you must never ask who I am, for I am your Emperor Joseph.'

Also unlike Bohemia, the country is wide open to the South towards Vienna and Austria proper. It was, in fact, the gateway to Vienna from the North and many battles were fought here, from the battle of Dürnkrut in 1278 to Napoleon's battles at Austerlitz, Aspern and Wagram; and as late as 1866 the Prussians were halted in Southern Moravia only by a hurried armistice and peace treaty. So the charm and glory of Vienna easily outshone that of Prague and national tension was hardly noticeable. What seemed impossible in Bohemia was achieved quite naturally in Moravia; German schoolchildren had to learn Czech and Czech children had to learn German. Political agitators who found such responsive audiences in Bohemia did not find agitation rewarding in Moravia.

The capital of Moravia was Brünn, Brno as it is now called, the Austrian Manchester, for most of the Monarchy's textile industry was concentrated in and around the town. The upper and middle classes were almost obsessed with cloth-making, mainly cheap cloth such as was worn by peasants and labourers in the Monarchy and in the Balkans. For the prosperous makers of that cloth wore only the best English worsteds themselves. And the 'United Fez Factories' produced a speciality, the 'fez', the wine-red felt flower-pot with a black tassel worn all over the Islamic world from Istanbul to Dakar, in Sudan and Persia, by the Sultan and by the last loiterer in a Tunisian village, and by the 'Bosniaks', the Austrian regiments recruited from the former Turkish provinces. Strange fruit from an unexpected tree!

Brünn was an old city, but, unlike Prague, had little to show for it except the fortress of the Spielberg, a hill overlooking the town. The fortress heroically withstood a siege by the Swedes in the Thirty Years War and so saved Vienna from much discomfort. But afterwards it became an ill-famed state prison where, among others, the Italian poet and revolutionary Silvio Pellico spent a few unhappy years of which he left a vivid description which reads exactly like *Fidelio*. However, those days, the days of the good Emperor Franz, were gone. In my time the Spielberg had become a tourist attraction where for a small entrance fee the casemates furnished with the usual torture instruments were shown without any derogatory mention of their long departed operators.

Biologists know more about Brünn than ordinary people.

Thoughtful visitors will discover a monument to Gregor Mendel, abbot of the 'King's Convent' in Brünn a century ago, who by patiently growing and crossing peas in his monastery garden discovered the laws of heredity. He subsequently wrote and submitted a short and humble paper on his observations to the Natural History Society in Brünn, where it remained unnoticed until more than thirty years later, and after the pious man's death it was found that those few pages contained the essence of the then new science of genetics, now universally known the world over as the Mendelian Theory.

Being only some fifty miles from Vienna, Brünn felt like a suburb of the imperial residence and its citizens prided themselves on being almost Viennese. Vienna set the example in all respects, in fashion, in the repertoire of the municipal and, of course, German theatre, in concerts and in the uniforms of the police. There was indeed a roomy theatre built by a firm of clever architects who in the 'eighties and 'nineties designed one type of theatre which fitted every place and climate. It was to be seen in Prague, Brünn, Vienna, Zagreb, Zürich and elsewhere. There was also a monumental Deutsches Haus in red brick with a concert hall where the Brünn Philharmonic gave its concerts and the most prominent Viennese actors, singers and conductors came regularly and honoured an audience which was equally at home in the Hofburg Theatre and the Court Opera in Vienna. The Czechs on the other hand had to be content with a makeshift theatre which also served as a makeshift concert hall. But they also had an 'organ school' where Leoš Janáček taught.

North of Brünn is Moravia's second largest city Olmütz, now Olomouc, then the seat of the archbishop and metropolitan of all Austria. Archduke Rudolf, Beethoven's pupil and friend and dedicatee of many of his works, once held the see and Beethoven wrote his *Missa Solemnis* for the archduke's enthronement, although he did not complete it in time. It would have been banned anyway.

Still further North were the coalfields and steel works of the Rothschilds, and Silesia—or what remained of it in Austrian hands after Empress Maria Theresa's war with Prussia.

If serious Austrians occasionally glanced uncomfortably at Prague, they had little cause to worry about Moravia and Silesia.

And Slovakia? As I have said, it did not really exist. Once

upon a time Western Slovakia had been part of the Moravian empire, but that was long forgotten. In my time the country to the East of Moravia and separated from it by the 'Little' and the 'White' Carpathian mountains was an integral part of Hungary, called Upper Hungary to distinguish it from the wide plains of the Hungarian interior. The Hungarians neither recognized nor tolerated any nationality or language other than Hungarian, although there were still some remnants of former German immigrants in the towns and more particularly in the mining towns where once they had found and mined gold. Up to 1919 the Slovaks had no schools and their language was half Hungarian. They had not achieved anything approaching urban civilization and what intelligentsia there was was brought up the Hungarian way in Hungarian schools and universities. The picture of a true Slovak was of a shepherd in the Tatra mountains, a barrier of wild peaks rising between Upper Hungary and Galicia, inaccessible for lack of roads and accommodation. This was where the 'gorals', the people of the mountains, lived, wearing broad-brimmed felt hats, rough shirts of home-made linen, close-fitting trousers and a cloak of rough, undyed wool called 'halina'. But this picture was, I think, a generalization, based more on imagination than on fact.

*　　*　　*

This, then, was the scene in the Czech lands at the end of the last century.

10

Prague, 1896

It was in that golden Prague of the hundred towers that I was born on a spring day of 1896.

There are people who say they can remember what the world looked like as seen from the cot or pram. I am not one of them. If it is generally accepted that human beings in later life never have it as good as in the cot or pram, it does not seem to have applied to me. Father and mother used to tell me what an awful baby I had been, crying day and night for the whole first year of my life. Perhaps it was an unconscious prophetic spirit inside me which registered its protest against having been thrust into the world without my consent. It was unjust to my parents. Nobody could have foreseen the troubles which were in store for all of us. I cannot remember this period of resistance on my part nor can I remember any particular babyhood bliss. Quite on the contrary. My earliest recollection is one of sheer terror, of the sharp, repulsive smell of carbolic acid, and of the bearded face of a bespectacled doctor staring at me and doing something to me which hurt. Strangely enough I remember his name: Biermann. Doctors' surgeries in those days were soaked in carbolic acid. Dr Biermann's house was no exception, and to complete the terror there were red and blue panes in the glass door of the dark entrance which made it look like the gates of hell.

With the vegetative rather than manipulated growth of reason I apparently gave up my useless protests and applied myself to my surroundings. I remember well the house where I was born, for we lived there for many years thereafter. It was fairly new, built in the bourgeois-palatial style of the 'founder years', the 'seventies and 'eighties of the last century. It was an 'apartment house' and our flat, like all the others, was rented from the landlord. There were only two flats on each floor and ours was on the mezzanine, higher than the ground and lower than the first floor, a little uncomfortable for the housemaids within and their boyfriends without. It was very well appointed. The rooms were large and high, the wooden doors were carved and had nicely embossed brass handles, the ceilings were stuccoed and in each room there was a tiled stove for burning coal. Beauty and usefulness were, I believe, still happily married. The double windows with Venetian blinds between the inner and the outer opened into the rooms so that it did not require acrobats or daredevils to clean them. The blinds played a trick which fascinated me in my early days. When I lay in bed and the room was dark except for the night light, a red-coloured glass half filled with oil and a little float with a wick which gave as much light as a small candle, the blinds worked like a 'camera obscura' and I could see the shadows of passers-by on the ceiling walking on their heads.

The large kitchen did not look like a laboratory as modern kitchens do. There was a large oven in one corner and a large table in the centre and only one or two stools. But neatly arranged on the walls and on shelves were all the rather primitive tools, wooden spoons and quirling sticks of various sizes, brass mortars, and coffee machines for grinding coffee, pots and pans; and in a large cupboard there was all the crockery and cutlery except the 'special silver' which was kept in the sideboard of the dining-room and used only when guests came for lunch or dinner. They never came to tea. There was no tea. Tea was a medicine for colds and indigestion and it was called 'Russian Tea', for it came from Russia. I remember the little metal boxes with Russian printing and a picture of dromedaries walking in the Gobi desert on the lid. The tea was compressed into tablets and, since it was regularly connected with some discomfiture, it was most unwelcome. English expert tea drinkers would not have touched it. The normal beverage was coffee although it was not drunk as compulsively as in Italy, Vienna or Budapest. The kitchen was a workshop for inspired brains and expert hands. Even the temperature of the coal fire had to be regulated without any mechanical or other aid.

In my early days we had paraffin lamps in all the rooms, beautiful porcelain bowls which needed much attention, and mother dealt with the wicks every morning herself. Later, gas lighting was introduced and father never reconciled himself to the thought that the house was filled with poisonous gas. He predicted that one day mankind would fall victim to its feverish quest for greater comforts. But the streets became more negotiable at night, and the man with a long pole and a light on top who ran at dusk from one lamp-post to the other was soon a popular figure.

It was often pointed out how much higher living standards were in England where even lower-class families owned their house with front and back garden. That was not the general ambition of Continentals. A house like ours was incomparably more solid and luxurious by pre-technological standards than even the majority of middle-class houses in England and a love of gardens in a country like Bohemia was effectively frustrated by the rigours of winter which no lawn could survive. But the pride of any Continental housewife, including my mother, were the cupboards full of monogrammed linen, of dresses and suits and shoes for all weathers. The maid did all the washing at home and special rooms were provided for it in the cellar and in the loft, while a seamstress came regularly and did the sewing on mother's sewing machine. One did not buy ready-made suits, coats or shoes but had them made to measure. I suspect it must have been a fairly easy life.

I I

The Sound of Music

The house stood on the left bank of the river in the district called 'The Little Side', perhaps because there was not much room between the river and the slopes of the high plateau which runs parallel with the Vltava and is divided into sections by steep valleys; the 'Petřín' or 'Laurenziberg', the 'Hradschin' and the 'Belvedere'. It was a corner house overlooking the main street on one side and a wide square on the other. One could easily see that it was the last house of Prague proper in that direction for at the corner stood a green-painted sentry-box and a few officials in green uniforms, each armed with a poker, stopped vehicles in the road and pedestrians on the pavement as they entered the city and if they found edibles they collected a tax. This unpopular tax was called 'akzis', a bowdlerization of the French 'accès', I imagine, because this tax was invented (and still exists) in France where it is called 'octroi', and the city boundary where it is collected is the 'barrière'. In Prague it was simply 'the line'. Peasant women coming to the open markets in town with baskets full of butter, eggs and curd cheese played an attractive game with the green-uniformed officials and I could see from our window how they succeeded in dodging them.

One side of the square on the other side of the house was occupied by monumental barracks, 'Albrecht's Barracks', so called after Archduke Albrecht. It was the only place in Prague named after a member of the arch-house and it was characteristically a military establishment to remind the Czechs of the iron fist of the victor of Custozza in 1866. But by then the archduke had joined his family in the vaults of the Capuchines in Vienna. Opposite the barracks was the entrance to the park laid out on the slope of the 'Petřín', and beyond the square the main street continued into the suburb of Smíchov, famous for the beer which was brewed there.

But to return to our apartment home. The housemaids of Prague are certainly among my earliest impressions; or, to be more exact, not so much the housemaids themselves as their singing, which may have influenced my whole life. Housemaids were easily available and Czech housemaids were renowned throughout Austria for their industry, their good temper and their singing. We called them invariably 'Marie', or 'Mári', which was the commonest name for Czech girls; but there were quite a few Boženas, Ludmilas and Anežkas among them. Mother had a great turnover in housemaids which may have had something to do with the barracks opposite. But they all had one thing in common: their songs. They came from the Czech villages and neither spoke nor understood German. But they had an inexhaustible repertoire. And they sang from morning till night, cleaning, dusting, washing up, beating the carpets in the courtyard or sitting on the kitchen floor working the dough. Of Italian folksongs it used to be said that they were a combination of soul and virtuosity. There was certainly little virtuosity in Czech folksongs. They were all soul. They dealt with the pleasures and sorrows of country folk; with the miserly master and the clever boys on his farm; with happy (but mostly unhappy) love; and with the favourite theme, the vicious stepmother and the abandoned stepchild (which is the underlying theme of *The Bartered Bride* and an essential ingredient of its popularity with the Czechs). The 'Máris' taught me their songs, the words, the tunes, and I still remember many of them. They brought the first music into my life and it was good music, too. It is a melancholy thought that the singing Czech housemaid has disappeared like so many other things and that the ever-ready radio has taken her place, that folksongs are no longer of the living but only survive mummified in folksong societies.

I had yet another early source of music which I remember vividly: the organ-grinders. Organ-grinders could be found in every city but nowhere in such numbers as in Prague. They were part of the life of the town, a guild with its own rules and code of conduct, loved by their audiences and supervised by the police. Organ-grinders were not allowed to play in the streets. They had to come into the courtyards where acoustics were better and street noises less disturbing. They were mostly old men, invalids from the Austrian wars, wearing on their patched-up coats the characteristic triangular medals with the emperor's effigy and holding an organ-grinders' licence in lieu of a pension; which was as economical for the taxpayer as it was a boon for a music-loving public. Indeed, organ-grinders had to hold a licence. This was no discrimination against this popular and meritorious company. The exercise of almost any profession or trade in Austria required a licence and certain categories of profession or trade could obtain it only on producing a certificate of qualification. This applied not only to doctors, lawyers, and chemists, but also to tailors, cobblers, booksellers, bricklayers, butchers, greengrocers. Those were the days of the expert and the craftsman and the authorities were anxious that the public should be served only by those who knew their job. I do not know whether organ-grinders needed a certificate of qualification or whether their infirmity contracted in the emperor's service was sufficient proof of their ability to turn a handle, but they served the public well and were certainly not beggars in any sense of the word. They were semi-artists, concerned with their repertoire, for they did not play the folksongs which every maid knew anyway, but arias, duets and choruses from the then current operas; and because the maids preferred sad songs, they chose the languid tunes of Bellini and Donizetti, 'Mira, o Norma', to 'Tu che a Dio', which, with their chains of thirds, had a strange likeness to Czech folksongs. And the housemaids would stop singing and listen enraptured to the lachrymose tunes of the 'flašinet' and when the organ-grinder had finished, pennies wrapped in paper would be thrown from the windows and balconies around.

And then there was music from the barracks as well. The band went and came often enough, leading the regiment to its exercises when every soldier was smart and well-groomed, and bringing it back in the late afternoon when the men were tired and bedraggled, but the band spick and span as in the morning. But more intimate and romantic sounds came from across the square—the 'Retreat' at 9 o'clock in the evening which summoned the soldiers back to barracks, and me to sleep. My parents probably thought that I was long asleep, but I often kept myself awake and, tucked into my warm bed, listened on winter evenings to this long, slow aria for a lonely bugle which marked the end of a day and, when a soldier died, the end of a life.

The Old and the New

As I grew up the town itself began to enter into my expanding world. The years of my childhood and adolescence are steeped in the sights of old streets and old houses with grey façades and roofs huddled together like old men and women whispering of other days, of palaces and churches, and of the view from the right bank of the Vltava with the Stone Bridge and the Hradschin and St Vitus Cathedral, which seemed to look down into every street and every window of the town. Sometimes I can still recall the musty breath of dark entrances and passageways and can see the snow nestling in stuccoed façades. Prague was no museum. It was alive. In the old houses people lived as they had lived four or five hundred years before, under the same low ceilings, climbing the same dark staircases, drawing water from the same wells in the streets. Only the fashions had changed; but life itself was as leisurely and as uncomfortable as it had been when these streets were laid out and the houses built in the golden days of Emperor Charles IV. Prague was indeed a place for walking, looking, thinking and dreaming like few other places in the North.

Father believed in exercise in the open air. But by this he did not mean sport. Nowhere on the Continent were people so passionate about sport as in England. We had to skate in winter, on natural ice-rinks of course, and many people, children no less than grown-ups, skated on the river which every winter was solidly frozen over. And in summer we had to play tennis and swim in the river. But all these sporting activities were only a pretext for being in the open air and proficiency in skating, swimming and tennis was of minor importance. Father, however, took an interest in the new game of football—new, that is to say, for Prague. There were two clubs, one German and one Czech, and they never met. But I remember well how, one

Sunday morning, father took me to the Czech club 'Slavia F.C.'
to see the real thing, the sensational début of an English professional team—Sunderland. In Catholic countries Sunday was
not observed as it is in England. After morning mass people
enjoyed themselves because it was their day off, and many shops
opened in the afternoon until, a few years before the War, it was
prohibited by law. Sunday was the day of sport and theatre and
every available type of amusement, including that football
match. And it was indeed the real thing! Within half an hour
the English, each one taller and stronger than their opponents,
scored twelve goals while the home side could hardly put a foot
to the ball. Thereafter the Sunderland men stopped shooting at
goal and gave an exhibition of dribbling, heading and passing
while the bewildered Slavia players and the no less bewildered
public stood and stared. It is different today!

However, this was quite exceptional. The normal exercise
was walking, at every time of the year and in all weathers,
walking as much and as far as time would allow. Father was an
early riser and made us all get up at 6.30 in the morning. By the
time I was ready to go to school he had already been to the
barber and had a little walk on the Laurenziberg. On Sundays
and during school holidays I was able to accompany him to the
barber first. O, the barbers in those days! There were a few
eccentrics who shaved themselves with that evil-looking blade,
but most men went to the barber every day at the same hour, to
the same barber where they were registered customers with
season tickets and friends. There was the master, Jirásek, with
half a dozen assistants and an apprentice, a boy with a large
bowl who splashed soap on the customers faces, so that Jirásek
and his men might shave it off and, with an alum stick, close the
wounds they had inflicted. The place had mirrors all round and
was full of chatting men with beards and moustaches which
needed daily attention. They all knew each other and Jirásek
and his assistants knew everybody in the district and beyond,
the latest deaths and births, political news and scandals already
reported in the morning papers and those not yet reported.
'Largo al factotum della città!' It was almost a place of public
entertainment with Figaro as the principal entertainer, and
after so cheerful a start to the day everybody must have gone to
work with real gusto.

When I look at the dull barbers of today, I cannot help thinking of those lively practitioners in the towns of yesterday. If the ladies had not come to their rescue the whole profession might have died not only for lack of customers but of sheer boredom. There were no ladies' hairdressers in the old days, but every morning an apparently impecunious lady came to do mother's hair. I imagine it was a clandestine profession.

After the visit to the barber, probably prolonged on Sundays, we often went up the Laurenziberg, not really a mountain but, as I have explained, the slope of the high plateau which runs parallel to the river and is cut into sections by a series of steep valleys. It afforded the best view of the town with the Hradschin and the cathedral on the left and the old town with its hundred towers on the right bank, the elegant curve of the Vltava and the bridges stretching like thin fingers across the water. It was, and I believe still is, a panorama of which one never tires. On top of the Laurenziberg stood a small replica of the Eiffel Tower which must have been intended as a compliment to the French who were such great friends of the Czechs. More interesting to us was the 'Diorama' next to the tower where for a few pennies one walked, apprehensive but fascinated, through a maze of mirrors to arrive eventually in front of the life-size picture of a battle scene made to look three-dimensional by some trick: Prague students and burgesses defending the old Stone Bridge against the Swedish. Father pointed out the defenders with red and the Swedes with blue sashes and the Swedish general, Königsmark, on horseback with white and blue ostrich feathers on his helmet. And he told me the story of that battle. On a dark October night of the year 1648 the Swedes crept into the castle on the Hradschin and the following day they tried to storm Prague. But the burgesses and students held them on the Stone Bridge, the only bridge across the river at the time. In fact, Prague was really saved by a despatch rider who arrived in the nick of time with the news that peace had been declared in far-off Westphalia. Whereupon the Swedes broke off the battle, stole what was worth stealing in the castle, and vanished. So the long war which had started thirty years before on the Hradschin ended precisely where it began and the battle on the Stone Bridge was the last and final action.

Indeed, the shadow of this war still hung over Prague. There were the baroque palaces of victorious imperial generals, palaces with grandiose façades and rows of half-columns like the Palais Czernin and carved entrances like the Palais Clam-Gallas and, most intriguing, the enormous Palais Wallenstein, intriguing because it was a ghost palace with windows blind with dust and its carved doors tightly shut, while the other noble palaces in the neighbourhood, Palais Fürstenberg, Palais Schönborn, were still occupied by their noble owners. In this sprawling, deserted Palais Wallenstein was all the romance and tragedy of that terrible war. The man who had it built was Count Albrecht von Wallenstein or more correctly, Waldstein, imperial generalissimo, adventurer and ruthless warmonger, feared alike by his master, the emperor, and by his enemy, Gustavus Adolphus, yet himself haunted by an obsessive fear of what was written in the stars. When, for reasons variously ascribed, he made overtures to the Swedes, he and his friends were murdered on the emperor's orders. A later descendant became Beethoven's protector and the dedicatee of the 'Waldstein' Sonata. But the family did not have the means to keep up so vast a palace as the one in Prague's Wallenstein Street. In my time it was slowly falling into decay. The stucco of the beautiful 'sala terrena' was peeling off and the garden, overgrown with weeds and with statues standing forlornly in the wilderness, was a sight of utter desolation, left untouched since the violent death of its violent owner.

The other living memorial of the Thirty Years War was the Stone Bridge where the last action had been fought. It was no longer the only stone bridge across the river, but it still was *the* stone bridge spanning the river with twelve lofty, massive arches, narrow and not quite straight, with stone parapets so high that as children we could not see the river and the exciting spectacle of long timber floats coming down with the current, two men at the head and two at the rear steering with long oars at the gap in a weir drawn across the river in order to give the slackening current fresh impetus. Stories were told of floats missing the gap and being shattered and the men drowned. The bridge was built in the fourteenth century, in the reign of Emperor Charles IV. It was guarded by huge towers at both ends, wedge-shaped towers characteristic of Prague. In Verona Goethe admired Sanmicheli's fortifications for their

architectural beauty which appeared to him as a symbol of the
spirit conquering the lower instincts of man. What would he
have said if he had seen these ornate, ceremonial towers? But
he travelled only as far as Carlsbad and never saw Prague.

The bridge not only spans the river. It also spans the gap
between the happy days of Bohemia's great benefactor and the
unhappy days after the long war. The planners of counter-
reformation who built the baroque churches also placed statues
of saints and whole scenes from the scriptures on top of every
pier so that obdurate Husites should run the gauntlet of this holy
company. These statues are not great works of art like Bernini's
angels on the Ponte Sant' Angelo in Rome, which the Prague
sculptors may have had in mind, but they gave the view some
picturesque contours and the saints fulfilled what had been
expected of them. Devout men and women crossing the river by
the Stone Bridge would make the sign of the cross and take off
their hats a dozen times—and a thirteenth time at a plaque let
into the parapet in the middle of the bridge. It marked the spot
where, in 1393, John of Nepomuk, father confessor of the queen,
was thrown into the river and drowned on the king's orders
because he would not betray the secrets of confession (to be fair,
he had other differences with the king as well). The long-
forgotten incident was rediscovered by the counter-reformers
and John of Nepomuk was canonized in 1726. This gave the
Czechs a more homely saint of their own tongue than distant St
Wenceslas and on June 21 each year there was a public holiday
and the sad event of St John's cruel death was celebrated with
fireworks and music on the river. I mention this story as an
explanation of the hundreds and hundreds of statues in Czech
towns and villages showing the saint in the same cassock and
posture holding the crucifix in his arms like a sleeping baby.
And as a Christian name John Nepomuk became popular not
only in Bohemia but in Austria and even in Bavaria.

The Stone Bridge afforded the best view of Prague, of the
river, the towers, the Hradschin, the whole romance of the old
capital, and all this free of charge, for the Stone Bridge was the
only one where one did not have to pay 'bridge penny', the toll
exacted on all other bridges from every pedestrian and vehicle,
irrespective of size, weight or age.

The Little Side on the left bank below the Hradschin was not as old as the town on the right bank but it was a distinguished quarter. Most of the palaces of the nobility stood there and the houses, built in the seventeenth and eighteenth centuries, had remained unchanged since. This was the heart of the German enclave in Prague, the last bastion of the former German majority. There lived the professors of the German university, judges, army officers and high civil servants, and apartheid was practised long before the term had been invented. In the streets hardly a word of Czech could be heard and the shopkeepers, though Czech, had to speak German, that special brand of 'Prague German' which was such a source of amusement to the Viennese. The houses had 'Conscription' numbers allotted chronologically rather than geographically which was most confusing for visitors but practical for writing an address. 'C. No. 1352, Prague' would have found its addressee without mention of any street. But the original owners were not satisfied with faceless numbers and the houses were known by their names and the appropriate emblem carved or stuccoed above the entrance: 'The Golden Stag', 'The Red Lion', 'The Bell', 'The Wheel', 'The Two Saints'. 'The Bell' in Spurmakers' Street was the house where I went to the kindergarten. I vaguely remember the kindly freckled face of the lady in charge and the boy David, a butcher's son, who for his elevenses always produced one of those Continental liver sausages with two little sticks at each end which made us other children with our bread and butter sandwiches envious beyond the proper innocence of our age.

Spurmakers' Street, steep and cobbled, ends on the Hradschin in front of the castle. To the left rose the Palais Schwarzenberg with its black and white *sgraffito* façade, very tall and rather forbidding. The princes of Schwarzenberg were not Czechs but the wealthiest landowners in Bohemia. The whole southern part of the country belonged to them. At Christmas we ate mirror carp, bred in their lakes at Wittingau. They had a more habitable palace in Vienna, behind the equestrian statue of that Field-Marshal Schwarzenberg who commanded the allied armies in the battle of Leipzig in 1813. But in Prague no Schwarzenberg had a monument and no square or street was named after them. Only this four-hundred-year-old palace represented the noble family in the Bohemian capital and I remember the portly doorman at the entrance in a gold-braided frock coat, gold-braided two-cornered hat, white gloves and a long staff with a gold pommel.

To the right was the Hradschin proper, the castle. The name derives from the Czech word 'hrad', 'the castle', and Hradschin or, in Czech, 'Hradčany', means a whole assembly or accumulation of castles. In a sense the description is not inaccurate. The work of generations was welded into one enormous building of various styles, half a mile long, sitting on the rim of the high plateau some three hundred feet above the town. None of those who had built the castle seemed to have been much concerned with architectural merit. The oldest parts had been destroyed by fire at various times and rebuilt in a hurry. Judging from its extraordinary size, it was not only the royal residence, but the accommodation for a whole government with all its servants, high and low. In my time it was empty, the blinds of the hundreds of windows were drawn and no flag fluttered from the flagstaffs. It was a ghost castle and the symbol of Prague's decline. Its last occupant was Emperor Ferdinand 'the Benevolent', who retired here after his abdication in 1848 and died in the castle in 1875. There could have been no more suitable place in which to disappear from the public eye. But no reigning monarch had resided here since 1612. And except for the Vladislav Hall and the chancellors' office with the two ominous and celebrated windows, there was nothing to see in that gigantic edifice.

It was also the girdle round St Vitus Cathedral. I said earlier that the Czechs loved Prague with an ostentatious and nervous love. Here, at the cathedral, one could understand why this was so. For that glorious Prague of old was not built by Czechs as Venice was built by Venetians and Paris by Frenchmen. At the behest of Emperor Charles IV the cathedral was begun in 1344 by a Frenchman, Matthew of Arras, and continued by a German, Peter Parler. When I was a schoolboy it was still as unfinished as the cathedral in Cologne, only the choir, transept and the stump of a tower having been completed. The front part was fenced in and through holes in the fence one could see a few lonely masons chipping away at yellowish blocks of stone with no visible progress. However, in the late seventeenth century the unfinished tower must have worried the church or other authorities and it was completed in a somewhat grotesque manner by putting a high baroque helmet on to the gothic stump. Strangely enough, the two incongruous halves had grown together as if they had been destined for each other from the beginning, or so it appeared to us who saw it every day. After the 'Collapse' in 1918 the Czechs speeded up the work and today the cathedral is complete although its personality is split not only by the baroque helmet which was left untouched, but because the new light-coloured half lacks the authenticity of the blackened old. But the old part is an outstanding piece of gothic architecture and decoration. The flying buttresses, reminiscent of Notre Dame in Paris, disguise perhaps more elegantly their structural purpose and the swing of their arches could not be more delicate. However, foreign visitors and art students were seldom seen in Prague and the beauty of St Vitus flowered as secretly as the beauty of the baroque churches and palaces down below in the town.

Under the cross vaults slept celebrities and dignitaries of the old kingdom. There is one chapel of particular significance, its walls covered with Bohemian semi-precious stones, an old wooden door with a bronze ring let into one of the walls: St Wenceslas chapel. In A.D. 929 the Czechs murdered their good King Wenceslas, in Czech 'Václav'. The wooden door is the door of the church in Stará Boleslav where the deed was done and the bronze ring is the ring to which the dying king clung when he was stabbed by his own brother. The king was a chieftain rather than a king and still a very young man at the time he was murdered—presumably on account of his excessive religious zeal. But he became the patron saint of Bohemia and inexplicably found his way into an English carol, and children today picture him looking like Father Christmas. When I went to school the chapel in the cathedral was still his only memorial, but it was rumoured that the most renowned Czech sculptor of the day was working on a monument which, a few years before the First World War, was duly erected in Wenceslas Square in the New Town. It shows the young and saintly scholar of twenty-six as an old warrior on an old war horse, stiff and expressionless and seemingly deaf to the words engraved on the plinth: 'Svatý Václave, oroduj za nás'—'St Wenceslas, pray for us.'

In the darkest corner of the old part of the cathedral, in a

metal coffin much damaged by time and neglect, slept a Habsburg emperor, Rudolf II, who ruled the empire from the Hradschin from 1576 until 1612, the last ruler to reside in the castle.
And here he lies, as it were, in exile. He was not admitted to the
Capuchines in Vienna where his father, his brothers, his uncles
and nephews are awaiting resurrection, for he did not behave as
a Habsburg emperor should and his coffin is no more neglected
than the empire was under him. But he is the embodiment of
another dark romance of the city of his choice.

He must have been a very strange man, highly intelligent,
highly educated, highly unsuited to a throne, to politics, or to
government. Indifferent to the fate of the living, he tried to get
to the roots of human existence by every means, through reading and thinking, through the arts, through magic. He collected
books. The nucleus of the Habsburg court library housed in
Vienna is the library of this strange man. He collected pictures,
every painting by Albrecht Dürer he could find, but also the
more sinister and scurrilous canvasses of the 'Inferno' Breughel
and even more dubious paintings by minor artists. The fate of
his collection was as sad as his own. Most of the pictures were
stolen by the Swedes in October, 1648, taken to Stockholm and
later sold by Queen Christina, Gustavus Adolphus' naughty
daughter, when she abdicated, embraced the Catholic faith and
went to live luxuriously in Rome on the proceeds of the sale.
What the Swedes overlooked was sold a hundred years later by
order of Empress Maria Theresa at interesting prices: Dürer's
famous 'Feast of the Rosary' went for one florin to the Strahov
convent nearby, some Breughels for 30 pennies each to various
buyers, and those which were unsaleable at the time were
brought to Vienna and waited under a mounting layer of dust
to be discovered another hundred years later and added to the
collections of other and more respectable members of the
imperial family. Emperor Rudolf also built the beautiful little
summer palace of the Belvedere in the Hradschin park, the
work of an Italian pupil of Palladio, with its open arcades and
patina-green roof, a real jewel such as Palladio himself had not
designed in Vicenza, Brescia or Venice. But no report tells of
happy feasts or celebrations around this palace and the 'singing'
fountain in front of it; and the emperor himself may have felt
frustrated when the arts and his books did not bring him nearer

to the mystery of life. So he shut himself away with magicians while the world around him slid deeper and deeper into the confusion of reformation and counter-reformation and his councillors waited in vain for decisions. Emperor Rudolf's chief magician was Tycho Brahe, a man of the twilight world of science and superstition and no ordinary astrologer. He was Danish but was obliged to leave his country when, around 1580, he announced that he had read in the stars that one day a Danish king would wander about the earth with nothing but a beggar's staff. Understandably, the Danish court took umbrage at such astrological indiscretion. That this prophecy was actually fulfilled in 1644 was small consolation to Tycho who was by then long since dead and buried. Emperor Rudolf eagerly secured the services of this rare man and gave him as an assistant young Johannes Kepler who, after Tycho's death, was no longer called an astrologer but was dignified with the title of 'imperial mathematician'. Tycho's task was to find the answers to the emperor's questions not only in the sky but also on earth. Behind the cathedral stood a row of little houses, dolls' houses, stuck against the crenellated old wall. In my day they were still inhabited and flower-pots stood in the tiny windows. For a modest tip you were invited to step inside and squeeze yourself through the narrow entrance down a winding staircase into the vaulted cellar with blackened walls and ceiling, and with furnace and bellows and glassware of more recent make. In the flickering light of a candle it looked like a real witch's kitchen. There, in the alchemists' houses in Alchemists' Street, under Tycho Brahe's supervision, men tried not to make gold but to brew the elixir of life. Tycho must have been an incorrigible optimist to his last day; and he lies buried in Tyne Church which towers above the Old Town Square on the other side of the river.

Tycho was a formidable magician. But the emperor had an even more formidable one, the High Rabbi Löw, the spiritual leader of Prague Jewry. The High Rabbi was to introduce the emperor to the secrets of Cabbala, to the occult life beyond our grasp. He created the 'Golem', the clay effigy of a giant, a robot with the cabbalistic sign of life on his forehead who kept the whole town in fear.

In my early days the old Jewish ghetto still stood, although the Jews had long since left and dubious people of all kinds had moved into the small dilapidated houses in narrow cobbled streets clustering round the Old Synagogue, the Jewish Town Hall and the old cemetery where the tombstones with Hebrew inscriptions seemed to follow their masters into the ground. We children were told that the 'Golem' was still about and his heavy steps could be heard on stormy nights when, in the old graveyard, he was searching for the tomb of his master who had left him behind with the secret sign on his head which nobody could touch and which would not let him die. The former ghetto was then a place of ill-repute although it may not have been as bad as some journalists pretended who thought that any self-respecting capital had to have a disreputable quarter of brothels, gaming dens and hide-outs for criminals. However, a few years before the First World War the whole area was razed to the ground except for the Jewish Town Hall, the Synagogue and the graveyard. New houses were built and new streets laid out, a new bridge thrown across the river and an extension of the Old Town Hall of the city erected. And there, in a corner, stood the awe-inspiring figure of the High Rabbi with flowing beard, conjuring from the dust his sinister robot.

Although then scattered about the town and country, the Jews in Prague and Bohemia—and Moravia—were an element of some consequence. They had lived in the country since time immemorial, and had had their regular cycles of alternate prosperity and persecution, so that at the time of their release from their ghettos they were neither unduly rich nor unduly poor. But they created an intellectual milieu which contrasted sharply with life around them. In Prague and in the towns they were doctors, lawyers and shopkeepers, and in Prague particularly they were the only really bilingual element. In the villages they kept the general stores and were often enough the only link between the peasantry and the outer world. I knew quite a few of these families who were devout but not orthodox. In the evenings parents and children would gather round the dinner-table and father would read to the family from the always handy volume of Schiller's poems or from *Des Knaben Wunderhorn*, so cultivating the blue flower of German romanticism which had long since withered in German lands. Gustav Mahler came from such surroundings and his music, I believe, remains only half understood without an appreciation of its peculiar roots. Indeed, the Jewish communities in Bohemia and Moravia bred famous men: Edmund Husserl, the founder of phenomenology, Sigmund Freud, founder of psycho-analysis, the pianists Ignaz Moscheles and Karl Tausig. The Café Arco in Prague was the meeting-place of Jewish-German writers who became prominent in German literary circles and beyond: Franz Kafka, Franz Werfel, Max Brod, Egon Erwin Kisch, the latter perhaps less known internationally, but an untiring discoverer of Prague, its oldest corners and oddest stories.

The Old Town on the right bank was no less romantic than the Hradschin and the Little Side. Its centre was the Old Town Square, perhaps not quite as wide as memory would have it, but very wide all the same, with no grass, no trees, and paved with hard, grey granite stones. It was flanked on one side by the overpowering façade and towers of the gothic Tyne Church behind a row of mediaeval houses with porticoes, and on the other by the Old Town Hall with another wedge-shaped clock tower, and a renaissance front with a balcony facing onto the square where, in 1620, the twenty-eight noblemen died. Crossed swords in the pavement marked the spot and after the 'Collapse' a bronze plaque with their names was added. What intrigued us children most was a large clock on the wall of the Town Hall known as 'Orloj'. It showed the time, the movement of sun, moon and planets as known or surmised in the year 1490 when a Master Hanuš constructed the clock which had a mechanism by which, every hour, two windows opened and the apostles with their symbols appeared in slow procession, each one turning a stern face to the onlooker. And when the last had turned away, a cock crowed and a skeleton representing death, an hour-glass in hand, pulled a chain which closed the windows and caused a bell to ring the hour while sun, moon and planets continued on their silent march through time. It attracted not only me, but every hour quite a crowd collected in front of the 'Orloj', for it had only recently been put into working order again after having stopped for four hundred years. Because of some serious disagreement with the town councillors Master Hanuš had taken away some essential piece of the mechanism which in the intervening centuries had never been replaced.

The Old Town Square, or Old Town Ring as it was called,

was the ceremonial place of the city. In my young days only a column in honour of the Virgin Mary stood in the centre. It was the memorial to the battle on the White Mountain in 1620 with its disastrous consequences for the Czechs. Small wonder that it was removed within a few hours of the birth of the new Republic. It was a symbolic act and meant no disrespect to the Holy Virgin. Indeed, the square was the scene of the most sumptuous religious ceremony of the year when on Corpus Christi day the archbishop, with all the clergy, the dignitaries of government and army, and the municipal guard in bearskins and Napoleonic uniforms, marched in procession round the Ring and High Mass was celebrated in Tyne Church, while the guards outside fired a general salute. In Vienna the emperor himself walked with a candle under the canopy behind the monstrance. Prague had to be satisfied with the general commanding Prague Army Corps. When the monument to Jan Hus was eventually erected on the Ring, few people seemed to realize the discrepancy between the past and the present.

That old square had, at least for us children, another significance. On St Nicholas Day, December 6, each year the Christmas Fair took place here, with hundreds of booths and forests of Christmas trees. With the snow already firmly settled it was a cheerful sight particularly in the evenings when in every booth the acetylene lamps were spluttering and the vendors, men and women, sang the praises of their wares, simple wares like oranges and apples, figs and dates, honey cakes and Christmas tree decorations of multicoloured paper garlands, glistening stars, candles and that artificial snow which mother detested because it clung to carpets and sofas as if glued to the fabric. But there was also an exotic touch provided by the vendors of 'Turkish honey', a mortarlike, sweet substance cut with a half-moon-shaped knife by men in Turkish costumes. They were not really Turks but 'Bosniaks' from Bosnia as their names Popovič, Ivančič, Djurkovič betrayed and they chanted in Serbian which was only partly intelligible. Much as she disliked large crowds of people, mother had to take me there once or twice but, to my great grief, she did not buy anything and I was not allowed to try this most desirable Turkish honey because the open market did not quite conform to her ideas of hygiene. But now and then I escaped with my nanny and had the time of my life, and bought honey which after all was not as enjoyable as it looked because it stuck to the palate. But nanny, being young, bought one of those paper balls with a rubber band which boys threw at girls and girls at boys and which obediently returned to the thrower. On St Stephen's day—Boxing Day in England— the fair was still in full swing though the forests of Christmas trees were much depleted, but by the following morning all the booths and people had vanished as if by some magic, and battalions of road sweepers were busy sweeping up mountains of paper, straw and twigs, a melancholy sight after all the noise and bustle; and next Christmas seemed far, far away.

From the Ring, 'Iron Street' where in the olden days iron-mongers had their shops and workshops led to the 'Carolinum', the building where Prague university had opened its doors in 1348 and which had not changed since. It was a building without any distinction except its age, but at one side there was a beautifully decorated gothic alcove and I was later to make the close acquaintance of the dark building and the vaulted hall to which this alcove belonged.

Opposite the Carolinum stood a building where one instinctively took off one's hat: the Old Theatre built in 1783 through the munificence of a Count Nostiz and where, on October 29, 1787, Mozart conducted the first performance of *Don Giovanni*. In Vienna all the old theatres had disappeared, but this one still looked as Mozart himself knew it, an aristocratic theatre with boxes all round, high and narrow. Well before the re-awakening of the Czech nation, Bohemian nobility had erected here its own 'court theatre' in opposition to Vienna. Noblemen like Count Nostiz 'felt' Czech but could not speak the language, and so the theatre was a German theatre and remained so until 1918. I remember many a memorable night there, from my first encounter with the opera of operas conducted by young Otto Klemperer whose long arms almost touched the proscenium boxes right and left, to the jubilee performance on October 29, 1937, with costumes and décor copied from the original designs of 150 years before, and with George Szell conducting. By that time the theatre had passed into Czech hands, but on this occasion cast and audience were mixed Czech and German and for one short evening the approaching storm was forgotten. I can still feel the chilly night air when, after the performance, I stepped out into the dark street and into the atmosphere of anxiety which gripped us all. Less than a year later I sat with George Szell in a Zürich hotel, he on his way to Australia, I on my way to London. . . .

Beyond the Old Theatre and the Old Town lay the New Town, the town the Czechs had built since the 'sixties and 'seventies when Prague began to grow. It had none of the charm and romance of the Old Town where every street and almost every house had a story to tell. The New Town only told the somewhat monotonous story of the new national self-consciousness. It was not laid out as generously as new Vienna nor was it as elegant as new Budapest. Only Wenceslas Square, very wide, one mile long, and with the imposing background of the National Museum, had any distinction as a design and as an ideal place for manifestations of both public enthusiasm and anger. The streets in the New Town immortalized the names of the re-awakeners and other national leaders and were, there-fore, no longer translatable into German. A new suburb was even named after the knight who started the Husite storm of unholy memory. For even the Young Czechs could not forget the nation's romantic twilight past and when on Sundays old and young paraded in national peasant costumes, the country-side seemed to invade the grey streets with the fading gaiety of those carefree days still celebrated in the 'sixties by the open-ing chorus of *The Bartered Bride*: 'Why should we not be happy if the Lord gives us good health?' The transition from such easy happiness to 'a land of hope and glory' was not without its melancholy undertones.

13

Pigs, 'Párky', and Pilsner

Our life in town was strictly regulated. Father's business, and school, were the main and inescapable regulators and father in particular was a kind of fanatic for order and regularity, doing—and making us do, as far as possible—the same thing at the same time every day, whether work, play or meals. It was his philosophy, the compass which kept us all on course.

We ate, quite naturally, Bohemian cuisine. There were restaurants outside Bohemia which advertised 'Bohemian cuisine'. But, to be honest, Bohemian, that is Czech, cuisine had little distinction and could not aspire to international acceptance. Having its roots in peasant life, like Czech society, it made the best of the most easily available produce of the land. Potatoes were the mainstay; not only the thick potato soup which is still the staple breakfast in peasant households in the villages, but potato dumplings filled with a thick, almost black plum jam called 'povidlí', a mixture of poppy seeds and sugar with melted butter on top; potato pancakes filled with the same 'povidlí' or, when the new potatoes came, in late August, just boiled potatoes with home-made curd-cheese and melted butter. In the fruit season there were dumplings filled with cherries, apricots and plums, always with poppy seeds, sugar and melted butter. Poppy seeds were a Bohemian speciality. Every peasant had a patch of poppies on his land, a mauve, cultivated variety which looked very pretty when in flower. In September the seed pods were neatly bundled up and hung under the eaves to dry. The seeds were then shaken out and ground before use. But I would not like it to be thought that the Czechs were a nation of opium addicts! These poppy seeds were quite harmless and tasty and the worst they could do was to produce a mild constipation if eaten in excess. Impatient mothers used them as lollipops for persistently crying babies at night.

Being of peasant origin, Czech cuisine made much use of flour and yeast, and yeast cakes of various shapes, sizes and fillings achieved a modest fame in the Monarchy. Czechs and Viennese alike called them 'buchty' when square, or 'koláče' when round.

However, the diet in town was not entirely or even predominantly vegetarian. Fridays were meatless days from tradition rather than conviction, but from Monday to Thursday we did have meat—boiled beef *every* day with monotonous and unchanging regularity. The tune never altered. Only the accompaniment varied. Bohemian forests yielded masses of the noblest of all edible fungi, cep or *boletus edulis*, which were dried and kept through the winter in muslin bags. They made excellent soups and sauces. Mushrooms were practically unknown. The art of cultivating them had not been developed then. Most of the year there was cabbage and savoy, sauces were made of onions and chives, and there were always, of course, potatoes in various guises. Eggs, however, were considered a luxury. Hens laid eggs at their and not at their owners' pleasure and, since they were scarce and expensive in winter, they were preserved when they were cheap and plentiful at Easter and during the summer. I remember how deeply hurt mother was when she asked an aunt of hers for the recipe of a cake and the heartless woman said: 'You won't make this cake, my dear, it needs eight eggs.'

Weekends were enlivened by a roast—chicken, duck, goose or pork, the latter traditionally with pickled cabbage, and dumplings as large as cannon-balls.

We were great eaters of bread and rolls and in my culinary recollections both have a place of honour. Only rye bread was eaten. Prague bread was quite a speciality and Prague bakers were artists of their craft. Loaves were round. One side was shiny brown and ornamented with concentric ridges, while the other side was a layer of flour. They were delicious. And the rolls! There was not just one type as in France, but half a dozen; pleated ones with poppy seeds or with salt and carraway seeds, 'mouth rolls' which looked like a pair of lips, 'emperor rolls' with several sections, croissants or sticks. The baker Odkolek had the best bread and the baker Vosátka the best rolls. They observed the old-fashioned courtesy of delivering their works of art to their customers' doorstep, even on Sunday mornings.

But apart from producing potatoes, poppies and flour, Bohemia was a pig-producing country. To rear the right type of pig in the right way was a great art and it produced the one culinary speciality which found its way into the menus of the most exclusive restaurants of the world: Prague ham. On my way to school I had to pass the ham factory of Antonín Chmel. It was not a factory in the proper sense, but rather a form of handicraft, and Antonín Chmel's oval stamp on the golden brown skin of a ham was as good as a hallmark on a silver dish. Prague ham was not too lean and not too fat. It melted in the mouth and it was a rare delicacy which made the hams from York or Parma blush.

And those rare Bohemian pigs supplied another dish which in the days of slow, unrefrigerated transport and general mistrust of preserves, was peculiar to and characteristic of Prague: smoked sausages in pairs, in Czech, 'párky' or 'little pairs'. That they were known internationally as 'Frankfurters' was simply one of the many injustices inflicted by Germans on the Czechs. In Frankfurt they were coarse, bulky and thick-skinned, while in Prague they were slim, juicy and tender. The man at the street corner with a little black kettle with hot water over a charcoal fire in front of him selling hot 'párky' with a slice of fresh bread and a pinch of grated horse radish was a common figure. There were hundreds of them in the Old and the New Town, on the Little Side, in all the main streets, and young and old, men and women could buy for fivepence this three-course meal of sausages, bread and horseradish neatly wrapped in white paper. Before the First World War people had already begun to complain about rising prices, especially if they affected their favourite dish. In fact, the price of sausages did not go up, but they grew smaller in size and people were amused and angry when the most widely-read Czech newspaper displayed in its window on Wenceslas Square a pair of sausages wrapped in a tram ticket. But, in fairness, a tram ticket in those days was a majestic document.

Food of whatever nature or quality needs drink to go with it. No wine grew in Bohemia. The great benefactor, Emperor Charles IV, who seems to have thought of everything, tried to grow wine on the hills south of Prague. The experiment failed lamentably through no fault of his, but the district which in the nineteenth century became a suburb of the growing town was still called 'Royal Vineyards'. And though the princes of Lobkowitz, one of the oldest Czech noble families, were still growing wine on their estates near the confluence of the Vltava and the Elbe which was sold in nicely shaped bottles ornately labelled 'Château Melnik', it could not compare with the produce of sunnier lands. In Prague itself we had a special problem with contaminated drinking water and typhoid was endemic. But the volcanic districts in North-Western or German Bohemia which produced the hot springs, also produced wholesome mineral waters and so we drank nothing but the famous 'Krondorfer' water.

However, the people, and the Czechs in particular, drank beer. They were expert drinkers and therefore expert brewers. The companion to Prague hams was Pilsen beer, the beer of beers known all over the world. Even in Prague it was treated with reverence and served in goblets instead of in ordinary beer glasses. But real connoisseurs would say that the beer from some of the small breweries in Prague was even superior to Pilsen 'Prime Source', or 'Urquell', or 'Prazdroj'. There were indeed many little breweries in Prague catering only for their special customers: 'U Šenfloku', 'The pretty snowflake'; 'U Štíky', 'The pike'; 'The Old Ungelt'; and there were dozens of other small breweries all over the country where the personal skill of the master and his men counted for more than chemical research and laboratories.

There were cafés in Prague but they did not play so important a part in the social life as they did in Vienna or Budapest. They were a rather German and Jewish institution and not quite in keeping with the Czech idea of sociability. There were proportionately more restaurants, a few elegant ones such as those in the Hotel Blauer Stern and the Hotel de Saxe where visiting archdukes or foreign nobility stayed, but most of them were popular places where one could have a good meal or just a glass of beer. And when, in mid-May, the sun shone warmly and the rain stopped, the open-air restaurants blossomed on the 'Belvedere', in the 'Stromovka' or on 'Shooters' Island' and on Sunday afternoons the bands played for those who were not engaged in politico-social activities; not only army bands but the bands of the postmen and the municipal fire brigade. I was still in the early stages of my musical education and bands fascinated me more than the unusual things which were put on my table. Sixty years ago the bands had a large repertoire; operatic overtures such as *Zampa, Si j'étais roi, Mignon, The Barber of Seville, Freischütz,* operatic excerpts, and, of course, selections and waltzes from the Viennese operettas. It could have taken a bandmaster only a few minutes to select a programme for a three-hour concert. Now, like all our musical occupations, band programmes have become a serious matter. When, not long ago, I heard the Venice Municipal Band in St Mark's Square, they played the Prelude and Liebestod from *Tristan,* de Falla's *Three-cornered Hat,* and the Ride of the Valkyries, all of which were played as well as any band could play them, yet still sounded hopelessly inadequate and rough. It was to me one of the minor, but no less warning signs of the many cul-de-sacs into which music has been running. For the light music of today is no longer performable by an array of forty or fifty wind, brass and drums. And flippant observers might say that the serious music of today is not performable at all. Have bands perhaps outstayed their usefulness? I do not know, but when we sat on 'Shooters' Island', their tunes, the clatter of glasses, plates and crockery and the buzz of conversation all round made a most pleasurable ensemble. And I watched the waiters serving beer and marking with pencil strokes on little round cardboard saucers the number of glasses the happy listeners consumed.

14

Three Months in the Country

Holiday travel was not yet the fashion. Father did not seem to need any holidays. But while I was still small, in the kindergarten and the first years in primary school, we spent the summer in a village on the Vltava about ten miles upstream from Prague, where father could join us every evening and return to town in the morning. The village was officially called Königsaal, for at some time in the past it had been a royal country residence of which no trace remained. There we rented a flat in a thatched house, a peasant's house. The Czechs called the village Zbraslav and there was only one Jewish family there who spoke and understood German. The man was a tanner and my parents used to buy leather from him, for in those days not only underwear and clothing were made to measure, but also shoes. There was no railway connection between Prague and Königsaal-Zbraslav, but only a dusty road and the river. The river was navigable from the first rapids, some twenty miles south of Prague, as far as its confluence with the Elbe and theoretically it was possible to have gone by boat from these rapids all the way to Hamburg. But in actual fact it was not. Steamers did not pass through Prague because of the weir to which I have referred before. The timber trade was more important than pleasure trips. But on the right bank at the southern end of the city there was almost a river harbour with landing-stages and steamers of various sizes, very small ones like Parisian 'mouches' for the local traffic between Prague and its southern suburbs; two medium-sized paddle steamers, the *Crown Prince Rudolf* and the *Crown Princess Stephanie*—they obviously had been so called by Old Czechs and the Young Czechs did not bother to change their names—which went as far as St John's Rapids; and there had been one large paddle steamer, the *Franz Joseph*, but ominously it blew up one day with some loss of life and was not replaced.

A fortnight before we set out on our summer holiday in early June, the flat in Prague was turned upside down. Carpets were rolled up, curtains taken down, all upholstered furniture covered over with dust sheets, white linen bags fastened round the lamps, and the whole flat smelt of naphthalene to discourage the moths while we were away. One day a furniture van arrived, and such furniture as was needed in our summer retreat, crockery and cutlery were loaded on to it, while the family, with a maid carrying the canary in its cage, took a hansom cab to the harbour and boarded the *Crown Prince* or the *Crown Princess*. There were no straggling suburbs. Once the chimneys of the brewery at Smíchov had disappeared, the countryside opened out on both banks of the narrowing river. It was not an exciting countryside except for one rocky spur which sloped steeply down to the river, the famous Barrand Rock of rare fossils. After two hours, entertained by the suntanned captain and crew, we arrived at the landing-stage of Zbraslav to be greeted by our host, 'pan', or Mr, Cisařovský whose bearded face and horny handshake I well remember. Pan Cisařovský was not a farmer. He was a peasant who worked his fields and tended his animals—cows and pigs, chickens and turkeys—and his orchard himself with the help of two young men and a housekeeper; he was a bachelor or widower, I believe, and they all lived together as one family. There were no farmers in Bohemia comparable to those English farmers who live in rather stylish houses and keep horses for riding and hunting. Pan Cisařovský's house was a cottage with a high, thatched roof and small windows and we occupied about half of it, a large sitting-room with windows on three sides and two or three smaller bedrooms. A large courtyard separated the house from stables and barn. The village itself was small, a cluster of similar thatched houses around the church, the inevitable statue of St John of Nepomuk, and the inn. There was no village green and no village pond, but the river was at the disposal of geese and ducks. The country around the village was flat and almost featureless. A little hill some distance away was planted with sour cherries which were just ripening when we arrived. On the other side of the river, connected with the village by an iron bridge, low hills covered with birch trees sloped down to the river like the tail end of a procession stretching far to the South and to the Bohemian Woods. Life and landscape were exciting enough for children of an age which was easily satisfied, the open fields, the sun, the chickens in the courtyard and the young turkeys which seemed to be easily afflicted by disease and needed all the attention of the housekeeper, the gathering storms which could be seen coming from far away. For us, all this was excitement enough.

Life in the village did not seem to have changed for many years. Every morning the village crier came down the main street wearing an old army uniform with shako and carrying a drum, summoning the villagers with a sustained roll and telling them the latest news, births and deaths, weddings and funerals, market days, cattle auctions, the arrival of a circus (as in *The Bartered Bride*). Without his drum he was the postman and, armed with an old sabre, the village policeman. The other important man was pan Klomínek, owner of the bathing establishment, a float with a few cabins on the river and a punt. He was the swimming instructor, ferryman and commander of the fire brigade, an elderly lanky man, seldom quite sober, but the hero of a terrible night of violent thunderstorms when lightning struck the house opposite ours. As its thatched roof went up in flames, pan Klomínek took charge, rescuing cattle and catching a bolting horse.

Almost every Sunday the 'šumaři' came, the typical Bohemian itinerant musicians, neither gipsies nor beggars but a highly respected band: a clarinet, a trumpet, a fiddle and a bass. In the afternoon they installed themselves in the garden of the village inn where the dignitaries, the 'starosta' or mayor, the vicar, the postmaster, the policeman and the old folk sat on wooden benches at wooden tables while the younger ones danced the 'beseda', the sequence of folksongs and dances which could go on for hours on end without stopping. Every 'šumař' had a glass of beer handily placed under his chair so that a short rest was enough for a long draught, whereupon one of the village children quickly replaced the empty glass by a full one.

Early every morning, except on Sundays, father went down to the landing-stage and at seven o'clock sharp the *Crown Prince* or his sister ship came round the bend of the river and took him to Prague and to work. Like all the regulars he knew the captains and crews and I believe the daily boat trip to and from Prague was his real holiday. In the evening we waited on the 'navigation', as the bank was erroneously called, and watched the funnel of the *Crown Prince* creeping slowly up against the current until the boat appeared in all its majesty and drew up at the landing-stage with much shouting and gesticulation.

The weather in Bohemia is not like England where its fickleness provides an inexhaustible topic. In Bohemia it was reliable and regular. Winters were cold and summers hot and there was just the right amount of rain. By the middle of November the first snowflakes mixed with the rain and by the middle of April the last ones saw the winter out. The 'March violets' blossomed in April, the 'three ice men' came in June, and all this was according to rule and to the hundred years' peasant calendar. Harvest started on June 29, St Peter and Paul's day, when the vicar, followed by the villagers, blessed the fields. At sunrise the next day and on the following days pan Cisařovský with his men and all the neighbours went to their fields, scythes on shoulders, and began to cut the corn. We could sit at the edge of the field and watch how the scythe in a wide semi-circle cut through the living stalks which fell as if with a sigh. The womenfolk gathered and bound the sheaves and a few days later the whole village resounded with the regular rhythm of flails in every barn. No echo of the noisy capital so near and yet so far away disturbed the peace.

And so summer went by. When the days grew shorter and the evenings cooler, potatoes were lifted and pan Cisařovský baked some for us in the hot ashes of a fire lighted in the field and no delicacy of Maxim in Paris or Sacher in Vienna could match the experience. One day in mid-September the van arrived again, our belongings were loaded on board, and the *Crown Prince* or the *Crown Princess* took us back to Prague, riding now more quickly with the current.

Later, when I went to secondary school and summer holidays were shorter, the family went further afield, to a village on the 'language frontier' where houses had tiled roofs and the main street and the village square were paved, where there were shops and a butcher who had rows of partridges strung up in his window. It was all German, more refined, and, compared with Königsaal, almost luxurious. The village was on the edge of the vast forests which stretched from here hundreds of miles into Saxony and Silesia. There were lakes large and small, long extinct volcanoes, regular cones of red rock rising from the plain and, a mile away, a station of the imperial-royal North-Western Railway. It was more interesting then the village on the Vltava but, strangely enough, the summers in Königsaal are in my recollection more vivid and happier than any other time of my childhood.

A few years before the Second Great War when I had moved to Vienna and came to Prague as a visitor, I took a boat, no longer the *Crown Prince* but a larger motor-boat, and went to Königsaal, now called only Zbraslav, in the hope of catching a breath of those happy days. It was a mistake. There were no thatched houses, there was no sign of pan Cisařovský or pan Klomínek, there were villas and restaurants, the river was regulated and a quai with a promenade and trees lined the bank. The old world had disappeared and even the village inn, still called 'U Vejvodů', had become a presentable hotel.

15

'Gaudeamus igitur . . .'

Although in a way it was sad to see the summer go and the days growing shorter, there were things in town to look forward to: school and concerts and the theatre.

Of course, I went to school. Everybody in the Monarchy had to go to school at the age of six and had to stay there until the age of fourteen. Today that seems an early school-leaving age, but then the hardships of life were accepted without much fuss. Unemployment was unknown, everybody who wanted to work found work without trouble, and it seems that everybody wanted to work.

Every country is and always has been convinced that it has the best educational system and the best schools, and Austria was no exception. 'Educational reform' was no topic, the concept of learning without tears absurd. Life was hard and school was designed to give children a foretaste of what they had to expect. The authorities did not worry about the happiness of children at school. The welfare state had not yet been invented, and 'happiness' was a matter of private and personal arrangement. The authorities flattered themselves that they neither prevented nor promoted it. This attitude did not result in widespread misery as modern philanthropists like to think. All hospitals were state hospitals, and neither asked nor needed any private charity. There were poorhouses and homes for the old and I do not remember any appeals for charitable donations. Every Austrian had a dual citizenship. He was a citizen of the Monarchy and a citizen of his home town, normally the town or village of his birth. And if he fell on bad times, it was the home town or village which had to take care of him.

School was organized on the same unsentimental lines and certain principles which today are the subject of much heated discussion were observed in a natural and unforced way. There were no public schools and no private schools. Only the kinder-garten was in private hands because it was not compulsory. But the owners and teachers in the kindergarten had to hold a licence and a certificate of qualification. All other education was owned and controlled by the authorities. Primary schools were com-munal schools and so were the so-called 'citizens' schools', three-year courses for those who after their five years in primary school did not go on to secondary schools. All secondary schools were state schools under the control of the Ministry of Education which set the syllabus, the date for examinations, holidays and all the rest. There were no school uniforms and no school ties. Children in Lemberg learnt the same subjects at the same time as children in Innsbruck. The idea that one school could be better than another did not arise. Therefore, parents had no choice. They had to send their children to the school nearest to where they lived, whether primary or secondary. Thus rich and poor, bright and dull found themselves on the same bench. It was all exceedingly democratic. Moreover, primary and citizens' school were free for rich and poor alike. Nobody had to pay for his basic education.

But there was one snag in this perfect arrangement. For those who wanted to go to secondary school there was an 11-plus examination and a very stiff one at that, including all the sub-jects which were taught in the primary school, religion not excluded. We survived. I have no unhappy memory of it. And there followed another snag. Secondary education was not free, although the fee was small, 40 Austrian crowns, about 30 shillings for the semester or half year. But parents who could produce a 'certificate of poverty' as it was heartlessly called, a certificate that they paid only the minimum income tax, were exempt from payment and their children could get their text-books from the school library. But there was no school milk, no school meals. Teachers in secondary schools were officially called 'professors' and they had no other duty but to teach. There were no head boys or prefects. Discipline was maintained by a book, the 'class book' locked in the professor's desk. There the professor noted every misdemeanour which occurred in his class and punishment was severe, 'carcer' or solitary confine-ment on Saturday afternoon combined with examination. If the sinner did not repent, he received the 'consilium abeundi', the advice to leave school which was not simply friendly advice, but an unfriendly order and could change the whole future of a naughty boy because no secondary school in the whole Monarchy could thereafter accept him. 'Behaviour' was indeed one of the many subjects which figured on our half-yearly certificates and was marked in the same way as any other subject: 'excellent', 'very good', 'good', 'satisfactory', 'unsatisfactory', 'totally unsatisfactory'. There was no points system to arrive at any of these nicely distinguished markings. It was rather a rule of thumb. As far as 'behaviour' was concerned it only meant behaviour at school. How we behaved outside was no business of the school but the sole responsibility of parents. School meant sitting at a desk working, school work, homework, exams both oral and written and nothing else. School started at eight o'clock in the morning and went on with one fifteen-minute interval until twelve noon when we went home for lunch. It restarted at two in the afternoon and finished at five, except on Saturday when it finished at one o'clock and the afternoon was free.

The type of secondary school which led to university was misleadingly called 'gymnasium'. It was a gymnasium for the mind and not for the body. There were no games or sports in any of the two (and later, three) types of secondary school. It was work and nothing but work. We had a multitude of subjects including the truly mediaeval 'philosophical propaedeutics', but no mention was ever made of music or the arts.

The sum total of this education was that we were, compared with English children, pale-faced, ill-mannered savants. That was, and I believe still is, the fundamental difference between English and Continental schools. In Britain people will talk quietly and queue patiently at a bus stop or a taxi rank. But on the Continent, in Vienna or Paris or Rome, the simple act of trying to board an empty bus together with two other people who for some mysterious reason want to be in front of you is enough to start a fight.

It probably sounds worse than it really was. As I said, I have no unhappy memories of school although my school days are buried under the debris of the misfortunes which befell us almost on the day I left school. It was usual for the 'old boys' to meet every year, privately, of course, for our old school, unconcerned with our future, had curtly dismissed us on the day we passed our last exam. But my former classmates never met and only one reappeared after the war. The others had either not survived or were scattered in the 'successor states' of the old Monarchy. But I do not think that we were downtrodden and robbed of all pleasure. Even at school we had some fun with professors whose weaknesses we soon discovered. There were generous holidays, a fortnight at Christmas, a fortnight at Easter, two and a half months in the summer, and the many saints' days observed in Catholic countries. There was time for private music lessons, for walking and reading. Everybody seemed to have more time. After all, we were not troubled by the suspicion that we knew better than our elders. We were a patient, docile generation content with illusions and, more important, capable of illusions. It is one of the great misfortunes of our century that the old docility and capability of illusion has not stood the test of two world wars. But it is equally true to say that our elders have not managed our lives too well. We were not brought up to know and recognize what we had to contend with. Should we then blame a younger generation which does not trust our unproven wisdom and does not wish to repeat our experience?

At the end of eight years in the gymnasium there was a moment of great tribulation, the final exam which was also the entrance exam for university. It was quite an ordeal, lasting several days and consisting of written and oral examination in all subjects, a good dozen of them. The reward for passing, as far as parents were concerned, was a traditional journey abroad and I have told the sad story of our arrival in and departure from Venice on the very day the First World War broke out.

University was the next step. And Austrian universities, too, were very different from English or American universities. There was no living-in at any Austrian university which had lecture rooms, laboratories, libraries and an 'aula' or ceremonial hall for ceremonial occasions, but no colleges, living quarters, sports grounds, nothing that did not serve the one and only purpose of teaching and learning. The debating and drinking and fighting clubs of German students with their 'colours', those who held their Sunday 'corso' on the Graben in Prague, were not sponsored by the university, but they adorned with their paraphernalia the yearly introduction of the new rector.

Although under the overall administration of the ministry of education, universities still enjoyed their old privileges. Academic soil was extra-territorial for the forces of law and order and the police were not supposed to enter any university building. Discipline was maintained by the rector and the decani of the four faculties, theology, philosophy (including all branches of science), medicine and law, and the 'pedells' or beadles. But at least in my time, order was never disturbed. Prague university was divided into a Czech and a German department, and though the two law faculties lived under the same roof in the old Carolinum and shared the same aula, there was peace and harmony. On the Graben, hardly a hundred yards away, the two factions bashed each other's heads in, but on academic soil Czechs and Germans met with cold but imperturbable politeness.

While parents could not choose a primary or secondary school for their children, the young man of eighteen or nineteen with the certificate of his final examination in hand could choose any of the nine universities of the Monarchy and could change from one to another as he pleased. He could not be refused, he had no applications to make, no interviews to attend. His certificate was his passport to university and all he had to do was to go to the 'quaestura' of his chosen university, present his certificate, matriculate—and pay. For university was not free, not even with a certificate of poverty. It was indeed rather expensive, particularly if it involved laboratory work. There were no grants from the state, from provinces or municipalities. Therefore, many students had to keep themselves by coaching others or working in banks or offices and for the sons of poor parents it was a hard time. But unless the student chose medicine or a scientific subject which required laboratory or hospital facilities, there was the time-honoured freedom of teaching and learning. There was no compulsory attendance at lectures nor were the lecturers, professors all, bound by the minimum syllabus set by the ministry. It was left to the self-discipline of the student to arrange his studies, get the necessary books or 'scripts' of any particular professor or examiner and present himself for examinations at the appointed times. Such freedom could be dangerous for the undisciplined, but it gave the inquisitive and ambitious the opportunity of attending a wide range of lectures outside his own faculty. I matriculated at the law faculty, but regularly attended the more exciting lectures of Philipp Frank, Albert Einstein's successor in the chair of theoretical physics, who explained the then still new theory of relativity; lectures on philosophy, history; and, last but not least, lectures on music while ·attending Karel Hoffmeister's piano class—later his master class—at the Czech conservatoire. I never felt more satisfied with life than in those first two years at Prague university with its dark corridors and vaulted halls of Emperor Charles' days. But the world was at war and one day in July 1916 I received the dreaded yellow letter from His Majesty who thought that the war could not be lost without me.

16

Two Cultures

I cannot say farewell to old Prague without recalling its cultural life which was as unusual as the Bohemian capital itself.

Nowadays there is a strong belief that cultural exchanges can make people forget their differences and mould mankind into one happy family. I would not dare to discourage such noble confidence in the arts though I cannot help feeling that in their present state they are not particularly helpful.

However, there was Prague, split down the middle politically, linguistically and temperamentally, and cultural exchanges were as easy as they could be, across the road so to speak. But they were salt rather than balm in the wounds. Nonetheless, running on double tracks, artistic life was more vigorous and more competitive than might have been expected in a city of Prague's size.

The Germans belonged to the German 'Kulturkreis' which gave them a feeling of superiority. But the problems of the Czechs were complicated and manifold and required a measure of understanding which they could not hope to find from their German neighbours. They were irritated by their past, they were newcomers who found all the seats in the cultural arena sold. They had performed a miraculous task by re-awakening the nation but now, re-awakened, they had to fight for a proper place.

In the 'founder years' of the 'seventies and 'eighties Prague, like Vienna, broke out of its mediaeval ring of fortifications and the New Town had to be built. Old Prague, as I have said, had been built by foreign architects. Now it was the turn of Czech builders to create the new Prague, not only private dwellings, but palatial edifices, the National Museum on Wenceslas Square, the National Theatre on the river bank, and the

Besedni Dům on Sophia's Island, the counterpart of the
Deutsches Haus. But there was no tradition from which to start.
Czech architects would not look to Vienna for inspiration.
Instead they went to Paris and looking round in new Prague one
could see the façades and domes of the Louvre, the Luxem-
bourg, the Invalides and the Paris Opera repeated in modest
and less assured imitations. The results did not impress the
world as did the monumental buildings on the Ringstrasse in
Vienna and the names of the architects are of little importance.

There were two prominent Czech painters at the end of the
last century, Joseph Mánes and Mikuláš Aleš, and I mention
their names because in their works all the romance of old Prague
comes to life. They were excellent draughtsmen, good colourists
but, like the whole nation, they were rooted in the past, producing paintings, drawings, and watercolours in the manner and,
involuntarily, in the spirit of the German romantics of the
'twenties and 'thirties of the nineteenth century. Nobody would
have believed that they were contemporaries of Cézanne,
Gauguin, or Renoir. They painted the murals in the National
Theatre where large gold letters above the stage proclaimed:
'Národ sobě', 'The nation for itself', meaning that the theatre
had been built without any help from outside and that others,
that is Germans, were unwelcome in its halls. The orator at the
ceremonial opening in 1881 summed up the problem of Czech
art after its long sleep. The theatre, he said, was a bright sign
of national pride bound by the spell of Krok's daughter,
Libussa. And then the curtain rose for the first time on
Smetana's festival opera. And Mánes and Aleš painted Queen
Libussa and her amazons, the knight Horymír jumping with his
horse from the Vyšehrad into the Vltava, peasants in their old
costumes dancing in the fields to the tune of a fiddle, a world of
fanciful nostalgia which bore no resemblance to the actual
world around. National pride and artistic purpose got in each
other's way and the world outside showed neither compre-
hension nor appreciation. But there was one artist whose genius
pushed up the blinds and looked into the future, Alphons
Mucha. But he found no friends in Prague and went to live and
work in Paris. Not so long ago an English art critic called him
the French founder of 'art nouveau'. But he was as Czech as
Prague ham and Pilsen beer.

Literature, which by its very nature has to be more articulate than the visual arts, found its problems even greater. There was no literary tradition either. The unhappy forgeries of Czech mediaeval epics discredited any attempt at looking for further genuine sources of Czech poetry. The poets and writers of the re-awakened nation had to look abroad like the architects. They wrote poetry and prose in the style of English, French or German poets and writers, they translated Shakespeare, Goethe, Schiller, Molière, Racine, Victor Hugo, Alfred de Musset, and gave libraries to the growing reading public and a repertoire to the National Theatre. They collected folksongs in the manner of *Des Knaben Wunderhorn* which was more genuinely Czech than all the translations and imitations. But the laurels of this early Czech literature belonged to women writers who were not as knowledgeable as the men and had the unspoilt gift of telling the stories of village and peasant life. Božena Němcová's *Grandmother* could be found in every Czech family.

But if, contrary to general custom, the reader would take note of the names of the librettists of certain Czech operas which have become known the world over, he would find writers of greater merit. The librettist of *The Bartered Bride* was Karel Sabina, one of the great hopes of new Czech literature. Like the women writers, he observed and listened to living people and told their earthbound stories. *The Bartered Bride* is *the* Czech national opera not only because the music is so Czech and so good but because the story, the characters, every word they speak or sing is so Czech and so true to life. But like everybody in this new Czech existence Sabina became entangled in politics, was unmasked as a confidant of the Viennese state police and died, dishonoured, in exile. The other Czech writer who served Czech music was Svatopluk Čech whose stories of pan Brouček were used by Leoš Janáček. Seeing him as I saw him when I was at school with his long beard and pince-nez one would not have credited him with any sense of humour. But his stories of a little Czech, pan Brouček, involved in all sorts of adventures on earth and in heaven are hilariously funny and typically Czech. However, if it had not been for music, neither Sabina nor Čech would have become known outside the small circle of their small nation.

In literature the Germans clearly had the upper hand. Their

poets, Rainer Maria Rilke and Hugo Salus were read all over the German-speaking world. They had the venerable Old Theatre of Mozart's days, while in 1866 *The Bartered Bride* had to be performed in the wooden 'temporary theatre', the only one the Czechs had at the time. When the new Czech National Theatre was completed in 1881 the Germans, not realizing that they were on the way out, built a still larger new theatre, the New German Theatre which was opened in 1888 rather fittingly with Wagner's *Meistersinger* in order to establish in Prague once more what in Hans Sachs' or Wagner's words was 'German and genuine'. So for a few years the dwindling German community had two and the growing Czech majority had only one presentable theatre. But, not long before the First World War, the Czechs again built a second theatre in the suburb of the 'Royal Vineyards', a few hundred yards beyond the National Museum on Wenceslas Square.

Similarly the Czechs had a rather small concert hall in the Besedni Dům where the Czech Philharmonic gave its concerts, while the Germans had the Rudolfinum with a large and a small concert hall and an art gallery. But again, shortly before the Great War, Prague municipality remedied the inequality by building a 'House of Representation' in the very centre of Prague which gave the Czech Philharmonic the large hall it deserved.

Such rivalry and double patronage benefited the arts. If in other respects the royal capital of Bohemia could not compete with the imperial capital of the Monarchy or with the other royal capital of Hungary, in the arts and particularly in music it was second to none. We were not troubled by much modernism. We heard neither Debussy nor Schoenberg nor Stravinsky. In the German theatre one could see and hear plays of the new school of 'naturalism' in literature, but in music Brahms, Dvořák and Richard Strauss were new enough for us.

If in other fields the Germans had the upper hand, in music the contest was more evenly balanced. Unlike literature and the visual arts, Czech music had never lost its tradition. Back in the eighteenth century when the Czechs and Čechy were forgotten, a stream of Czech musicians emerged from Bohemia. There must have been quite a few itinerant music-makers among them, 'Bohemians' of Henri Murger's definition like the 'šumaři' who still roamed the Czech countryside when I was young. But those recorded by history were highly respectable such as the Benda brothers from Staré Benátky, František the violinist and founder of the 'Berlin school of violin playing', and Jiří or George, one of the most successful composers of operas and 'melodramas' of his time. Václav Štamic from Německý Brod was the moving spirit of the famous Mannheim orchestra, Jan Ladislav Dusík from Časlava, more often called Dussek, became Talleyrand's chamber pianist and we still played his rondos, 'Les Adieux', 'La Consolation', 'La Matinée', with their easy brilliance totally unrelated to the title. Nor should we forget Joseph Mysliveček, a miller's son who went to Italy where he called himself Giuseppe Venturino, 'the little huntsman', an exact translation of his Czech name, scored resounding successes both with his operas and with the prima donnas, was called 'il divino Boemo', the divine Bohemian, was met and admired by Mozart, genius, libertine and spendthrift who after all the furore died miserably in great poverty. Czech musicians were still travelling abroad in the early days of the 'Re-awakening'. In Beethoven's day Vienna was full of them.

But since the 'Re-awakening', Czech musicians no longer left their country for good. Smetana spent a few years in Sweden but returned to Prague; and so did Dvořák. Joseph Proksch was already dead when I had my first piano lesson but I learned after his method which was still famous—he had been Smetana's teacher. At the Czech conservatoire there was Otakar Ševčík, one of the most renowned violin teachers of all time, and pupils came to him from all over the world. His best pupil, Jan Kubelík, was among the greatest violinists and so was František Ondříček for whom Dvořák had written his violin concerto. The Bohemian String Quartet with Karel Hoffman at the first violin and the composer Joseph Suk at the viola desk rivalled the great quartet ensembles of the time, the Brussels, Rosé, Joachim and Gewandhaus Quartets. All this was worthy of the great past when Mozart, Beethoven, Weber, Berlioz, Wagner, Liszt and Brahms came to Prague. The two hundred-year-old impetus of Czech musical life was still strong and the Czechs knew it. The Germans in Prague had nothing similar to offer.

In those pre-radio, pre-gramophone days music was almost a different art from what it is now. Those who loved it, the 'amateurs' in the real sense of the word, were much closer to it. By playing an instrument themselves they had a much more intimate knowledge of the music they heard. The orchestras were probably not as good as they are now. When I hear Beethoven's Eighth Symphony played now with consummate ease, I am reminded of the wobbly horns I used to hear in the minuet when I first went to concerts. But such imperfection appeared as a human touch appreciated rather than resented. On the other hand the virtuosity of 'virtuosos', as they proudly called themselves, was savoured with greater expertise. Violin, piano or song recitals were much more frequent and popular than they are nowadays, for they allowed a much closer contact between the artist and the public. I remember innumerable recitals when, after the official programme, half the lights in the hall were turned off, hundreds of true connoisseurs and enthusiasts gathered round the platform, and another recital of encores began, Kubelík, Huberman or Ysaÿe playing real virtuoso pieces, Paganini's 'Streghe', Sarasate's 'Gipsy Tunes' or a great favourite, the 'Scherzo' by Daniel van Goens; or young Moriz Rosenthal at the piano playing Johann Strauss's 'Blue Danube' with the right hand and 'Tales from the Vienna Woods' with the left hand; or Tetrazzini singing Adolphe Adams coloratura variations on 'Ah, vous dirais-je, maman'; astonishing exhibitions of sheer virtuosity, certainly of little musical value, but leaving us who knew the technical difficulties in a state of wild exhilaration. Music did not have the controlled dignity it has today when virtuosity for its own sake is discredited, but it had, I believe, more blood in its veins.

Familiarity with the art and the artist persisted also in the opera house. When I think of the impoverished repertoire today, I cannot help feeling sad. Was it all really so bad what we heard? Boieldieu's *Dame Blanche*, Adam's *Postillon de Longjumeau*, Kreutzer's *Nachtlager in Granada*, Bellini's *Norma* and *Sonnambula*, Donizetti's *Don Pasquale*, *Lucrezia Borgia*, *Lucia di Lammermoor*, Meyerbeer's *Huguenots*, *Le Prophète*, *Robert le Diable*, Gounod's *Romeo and Juliet*, Ambroise Thomas's *Mignon* and many others? There was not the insensitive, learned approach of today. I still have the beautifully bound copy of the vocal score of *Don Giovanni* which my parents gave me sixty years ago. It was published in 1901 and the arranger said in a foreword that he had added the 'secco' recitatives 'because they were slowly replacing the spoken dialogue' and at the end of the first part of the second finale, when Don Giovanni disappears amid flames and destruction, the arranger remarked: 'If contrary to practice the following scene (the second part of the finale) is sung, the hall is not to be destroyed.' But this is precisely how I heard *Don Giovanni* in the years before the Great War, with spoken dialogue, without the second part of the finale and with other no less barbarian cuts. Indeed, one was not fussy but determined to enjoy oneself. For that reason, too, operas were sung in the language people could understand. The Czech National Theatre performed the whole *Ring* in Czech. Even after the war I heard the whole cycle at the Scala in Italian conducted by Toscanini. The idea of singing an opera in the original language would not have occurred to anybody. When Caruso came, he sang in Italian while the rest of the cast sang in German or Czech as the case may have been, and it did not mar the pleasure.

Also the behaviour of the audience in the opera house might today be called irreverent. Applause after a well-sung aria was expected and welcome and encores were freely granted irrespective of dramatic continuity, Don Giovanni's 'Champagne Aria' no less than the Duke of Mantua's 'la donna è mobile' or Walther von Stolzing's Prize Song.

All the arenas of music in Prague are hallowed in my memory, the National Theatre no less than the New German or the Old Theatre, the concert hall in the Besedni Dům and the halls of the Rudolfinum. They are all connected with those irretrievable and unrepeatable first impressions, first meetings and first hearings. The National Theatre was the first I saw from inside and I can still feel the excitement at the first rising of the curtain. It was a fairy-tale, one of the frequent children's performances on Sunday afternoons. In the New German Theatre I saw my first opera, Weber's *Freischütz* and for a long time afterwards Samiel and Caspar disturbed my sleep.

Certain operas had to be heard at the National Theatre, above all *The Bartered Bride* which was played almost every Sunday afternoon or evening. I well remember the coloured posters with the famous bass Heš as Kecal on the occasion of the 1,000th performance. But Smetana's seven other operas and Dvořák's nine operas were also regularly played. The German opera never attempted any of them, understandably so for the Czechs had the authentic style and the authentic language. In deference to current political ideas the National Theatre also cultivated the Russian operatic repertoire: works by Glinka, Balakirev, Mussorgsky, Rimsky-Korsakov, Borodin and Tschaikovsky, which it was virtually impossible to hear anywhere else outside Russia. But apart from such concessions there was no discrimination in the repertoire of the Czechs; German, Italian and French operas were performed, all in Czech. Some famous singers came from the National Theatre and some stayed there. We went to hear *Götterdämmerung* in Czech because of the National Theatre's Brünnhilde, Alžběta Morfová, a gigantic woman with a gigantic voice. The jokers on the Vltava used to say that she could not see a cup of coffee on the table in front of her. Others made international careers, like the brothers Karel and Emil Burian, one becoming an 'imperial-royal Kammersänger' at the court opera in Vienna, the other a 'royal Kammersänger' at the court opera in Dresden. When they returned to Prague as guests for a few evenings they sang, of course, only at the National Theatre.

But the German Theatre had a distinction which the National Theatre could nor emulate and that was due to its director Angelo Neumann. Angelo Neumann's name appears in every biography of Wagner. He was the man who, with Wagner's approval and support, loaded the whole *Ring*, cast, orchestra, scenery, machinery and costumes on to his Thespis cart and performed the reputedly unperformable tetralogy all over Europe, from St Petersburg to Paris and from Stockholm to Palermo, and made his peripatetic 'Richard Wagner Theatre' a legend. His pioneering task completed, he retired to the calmer waters of the German Theatre in Prague, a great organizer, a rare discoverer of talent and a dauntless showman, in short the perfect theatre director. Almost all the famous German actors and singers of the time had served an apprenticeship under his direction. Among conductors Gustav Mahler, Karl Muck, later 'Generalmusikdirektor' in Munich, Leo Blech, later 'Generalmusikdirektor' in Berlin, and Otto Klemperer earned their first laurels in Prague. The great international operatic stars, Caruso, Arimondi, Battistini came regularly to the New German Theatre and I remember the début of Alfred Piccaver as the

Duke in *Rigoletto* when the New German Theatre was full of Czechs, for Alfred Piccaver had been hailed as the new Caruso.

But Angelo Neumann's trump card were the 'Mai-Festspiele'. It sounds almost unbelievable that there were no music festivals in those days except Bayreuth, which was strictly confined to Wagner. The idea of an annual opera and drama festival was Angelo Neumann's own and the month of May was the ideal time. The best singers and actors from all over the world assembled in Prague, whole ensembles like the then famous corps de ballet of the Paris opera came, and on May 1 before the first festival performance a fanfare sounded from the balcony of the New German Theatre which could be heard all over the town. The centre piece of the festival was, not surprisingly, the *Ring* with the Bayreuth cast, some of whom had sung their parts under Wagner's own supervision. It was on such an occasion that I heard it for the first time and disliked it. But the festival was by no means another Bayreuth. There was always a Mozart cycle and I will never forget my first encounter with the *Entführung aus dem Serail*, not only because of the experience itself but because of what happened immediately afterwards. As we left the theatre special editions of the evening papers were being sold in the streets, reporting that Vesuvius had erupted and killed thousands in the villages on its slopes. The year was 1908.

For that month of May, German Prague once again dominated. But in 1910 Angelo Neumann died. His successor, a routinier without Neumann's spark, tried hard to keep up the reputation of the German Theatre and of the May Festival. But its star had set. The German minority took refuge in the commonplace consolation that nobody was irreplaceable, but Neumann was. Despondency spread among the German community. The days of German Prague drew to their end.

17

A Short Walk in the Fresh Air

I came back to Prague at the beginning of November, 1918, after an adventurous journey from the Russian front, still wearing the uniform of the Imperial and Royal Field Artillery Regiment No. 9, but without the emperor's cockade on my cap. The town—and the nation—were celebrating, a red, white and blue flag fluttered from the Hradschin, the castle had come to life. But I had no time for celebrations. I hurried back to the university and to the conservatoire which was soon to become a State conservatoire. After two years of hard work during which there was little visible change in Prague except that the Czechs seemed to be noisier and the Germans quieter, I found myself in the aula of the Carolinum to receive my doctor's diploma.

Austrian, like German, universities were sometimes sarcastically called 'doctor factories'. The truth of the matter was that the doctor's degree was the only one a university could confer, whether 'doctor divinitatis', 'doctor medicinae', 'doctor philosophiae' or 'doctor utriusque iuris'. There were no intermediate titles. The freshman was simply called 'studiosus' and the undergraduate who had passed his first examinations was no more than a 'candidatus' and both these titles indicated the temporariness of his status and were unsuitable for a visiting card. The 'studiosus' who did not become a 'candidatus', and the 'candidatus' who did not become in good time a 'doctor', had simply wasted his time and had nothing to show for it. And heavens knows, it was a hard slog to get that far with little guidance or advice.

But here I was in the aula with half a dozen other 'promovendi', without any outward sign of my new dignity, facing the rector and the professors of the German law faculty surrounded by the beadles, all in sumptuous mediaeval robes. The rector addressed us in Latin, shook hands with us while obviously thinking of something else, and handed each of us a large parchment with the seal of the 'alma mater Carolo-Ferdinandea' headed by the five letters 'Q.F.F.F.S.', 'quod felix, faustum, fortunatumque sit' with which the Roman Senate used to address the Roman people. And this parchment, all in Latin, confirmed that the 'illustrissimus vir' had received his doctor's degree 'sub auspiciis imperatoris'. The year was 1921 and the 'imperator' was no more, but the German university in Prague did not seem to have been informed of the change.

I well remember that day when, after the promotion ceremony which in fifteen minutes rounded off my twenty years at school, I stepped out of the old Carolinum into the hesitant sunshine of a March morning, into a new Prague, a new world. In ordinary times that should have been a moment of satisfaction, a pause to take a deep breath before starting a life's career. But now there was an air of unreality which obscured my view of the future.

My thoughts turned back to the fateful days of 1914. In 1908 the Czechs revolted on behalf of the Serbs. When on June 28, 1914, Archduke Franz Ferdinand and his wife were shot by a Serb patriot, they held their breath. An unacceptable ultimatum was delivered by the Austro-Hungarian ambassador in Belgrade—and there was not a stir in Prague. War was declared, and the Czechs obediently joined the colours. They did not even seem to notice that their political leaders were arrested and sent to some distant prison. The good soldier Švejk slipped unrecognized into the emperor's coat—and out of it. In Galicia he went over to the Russians, at home he misdirected troop and ammunition trains, cut telephone lines in innocent error, and left vital mail undelivered. I had met him in many disguises, with the regiment back in Southern Bohemia and out in the desolate wastes of Eastern Galicia. Everybody knew him and his pranks, but he was such a likeable fellow that nobody spoilt his game. The newspapers and communiqués did not mention it, but the whisper went round that Professor Thomas Garrigue Masaryk was abroad and was doing great things for the nation, the same man whose voice had long been drowned by the now silenced cries of wilder nationalists. But he could not delude himself that the Habsburg monarchy would survive. He had never aimed at its destruction, but he felt that it was his duty to prepare for the inevitable. He organized the tens of thousands of Czech deserters in Russia. And their long trek through Siberia to the China Sea and to a boat which could bring them back to Europe and to a triumphant entry into liberated Prague was their only epic. Even at this crucial time, when history wore a forced smile for the Czech people, it could not bring itself to give them the glory of which later generations would tell with pride. After all their age-long troubles, independence fell into their lap like an over-ripe fruit. And then Masaryk himself returned, the liberator. And he at once put the brakes on the enthusiasm. He knew how delicate this over-ripe fruit was, what infinite care it needed if it was to be enjoyed. There were no excesses, no persecutions, no German schools were closed, German Bohemia remained German as before. But the Germans were irreconcilable, implacable, unforgiving. For all its unfriendliness, the hand of the Viennese government had been a protecting hand. Now the Czechs were alone.

When I walked away from the Carolinum on that day in March, 1921, all these thoughts followed me through the familiar streets of old Prague. It was still the old Prague, only here and there a new and modern house was being built and the new affluence was mirrored in happy faces, bigger shops, louder bustle. At the once deserted gates of Hradschin castle there now stood a guard of honour in new uniforms and the professor of philosophy ruled the happiest of all the successor states. Who could have thought that twenty years was all that fate had to spare for the Czechs?

Valedictory

Such were some of the strange and fascinating people among whom I was born and spent the first half of my life. It cannot be easy for English-speaking people to understand the anomalies and absurdities, the grandeurs and miseries, of the old multi-national, multi-lingual empire, nor to comprehend the sense of personal tragedy as successive tidal waves of war or political 'adjustment' swept frontiers aside and then, as the waters receded, left families and friends divided and stranded, often on alien and improbable shores.

The two maps on pages x and xi are eloquent enough; but they do not tell the whole story. I should, perhaps, have added a third, dated 1971. For that would have shown the effects of the greatest of all tidal waves; and when those waters receded, they left Austria as a lonely promontory, washed to the North and East by a Red Sea more sinister and ruthless than all the Huns and Avares.

Tu, felix Austria? I wonder.